The Secret Diary of a Superwoman

A Journey of Ideas, Insights and Inspiration Through
the Personal and Business Evolution of an
Entrepreneur on a Mission to Take as Many Women
With Her as Possible

Vicki Irvin

Publisher: Vicki Irvin Enterprises,
6333 Old Branch Avenue, Suite 303, Temple Hills MD 20748

While they have made every effort to verify the information
provided in this publication, neither the author nor the publisher
assumes any responsibility for errors in, omissions from or
different interpretation of the subject matter.
The information herein may be subject to varying laws and
practices in different areas, states and countries. The reader
assumes all responsibility for use of the information.

ISBN-13:
978-1490352565

ISBN-10:
1490352562

This book is dedicated to my mother-in-law Rosalee Irvin who continues to defy all odds.

Her strength, resolve and passion for life remain a constant source of inspiration and motivation for me to do more and be more in life.

Everyone deserves a cheerleader like her!

ABOUT VICKI IRVIN

Vicki Irvin is an entrepreneurial and business coach for women looking to go to the next level in life.

She has worked with thousands of people on how to build a better business and recognize the life they were born to live.

Her Superwoman Lifestyle community has thousands of followers across the country and her work has been included or featured by several media outlets including:

Essence Magazine, USA Today, Bloomberg Radio, Lifetime TV, CNN's HLN, Millionaire Blueprint Magazine, Fit Figures Magazine, Who's Who of Women Entrepreneurs, and the Investor's Business Daily.

Having worked in corporate America as a Human Resources professional and been witness to hundreds of people losing their jobs, Vicki stepped away from her traditional 9-5 job in pursuit of a more stable way to secure her financial future.

After discovering the blueprint to winning in business, she went on a mission to teach others how to turn their passions to profit and take back control of their lives.

Visit us at **www.SuperWomanLifestyle.com** to join thousands of progressive women like yourself and become part of this phenomenal movement that is transforming lives in Business, Beauty & Balance one day at a time.

WHAT PEOPLE ARE SAYING ABOUT VICKI

I was thrilled to be a speaker at Vicki Irvin's Extreme Women Entrepreneurs Event, it was amazing!
I have great admiration and appreciation for women in the business world who have not allowed their life dreams, goals and potential to be denied by their gender. I look forward to working with Vicki again.

Stedman Graham
CEO Graham & Associates

I have loved working with Vicki in her Mastermind group over the course of the year! She has been a supportive mentor and coach that made me do the things in business I was running away from which are the things that lead to REAL profit. The accountability system she has in place is priceless and forced me to rise to the occasion every time.

Valerie Sherrod
The 90-Day Author
www.The90DayAuthor.com

I had an amazing time performing at Vicki's Extreme Women Entrepreneurs Event!
I met some smart women with some amazing businesses and was blown away by the level of knowledge in the room! If you are a woman in business, this is THE place to be!

Chante Moore
R&B Recording Star

I had a great time at Vicki's event. I love what she is doing with women entrepreneurs, it was important to me to always have my own thing. I am all for women in business fulfilling their passions.

Jennifer Williams
Entrepreneur & Reality TV Star

Vicki Irvin is one of the smartest marketers I have ever met! What I learned from her in just a couple of meetings would have taken me an enormous amount of time and wasted money to learn on my own. She not only helped me brand, but also gain clarity on my Signature System, that I had been using for years, but not even realizing I had one! I am blown away by the amount of info that I didn't realize was so important for an entrepreneur to make money! I'm more excited than ever about my business.

Cindy Cohen
Certified Professional Success Coach

If you have lots of ideas for a business and you don't know where to start, do not let anything or anyone get in your way to learn how to create and monetize your brand with Vicki Irvin – who is sincere, successful and smart! With Vicki's help, I am focused, I have a brand and I have a system that is already opening doors to increasing my wealth and to helping others.

Willetta Love
Founder, Embrace With Love
www.EmbraceWithLove.com

INTRODUCTION

When I wrote my first book – *"The Superwoman Lifestyle Blueprint"* – I wanted to help as many women as possible discover how to unleash the Superwoman within them.

I am very excited and encouraged by the feedback I got to that book and by some of the stories many fabulous women have shared with me about how they implemented what I shared.

I love hearing stories of how these ideas have changed women's lives in many different ways.

As I said in the introduction to that book, a Superwoman enjoys a fulfilling life when she is able to experience the following:

- Financial independence
- Rewarding business or career
- Great relationships
- Happy and healthy family
- Time for your closest friends
- Me time

That first book was not just about theory. It was a practical guide packed with suggestions, ideas and exercises about changes you can make in the way you live.

In fact, I subtitled it *"The Ultimate Woman's Guide to Embracing Her Strengths, Defining Her All, and Living the Life She Was Born to Live in Business, Beauty & Balance."*

When I've been chatting with hundreds of women as I work with clients, attend events around the country and travel all over the world, many have asked me for more specific stories and examples of how I apply these ideas every day in all aspects of my life.

The Daily Reality

That feedback encouraged me to keep a diary and share with you the day to day reality of how I live my life and apply the Superwoman concepts every day.

My idea was to keep a note of what I was experiencing and to show how being a Superwoman is not some fancy theory but is something practical that touches everything we do each day.

So this book is my diary and here's what you'll find inside:

- Quotes that inspire me

- Daily experiences from my life – personal and business – that show you how I apply these ideas to everything that I do

- Regular actions you can take to make sure you get the Superwoman habit

I've not pinned the entries down to specific dates because I want you to be able to pick it up and follow it at any time rather than waiting for specific days or months.

Of course, I'm not saying there's anything special about me and my life. I'm certainly not perfect.

As you'll see I have my good days and bad days like everyone.

In fact, one of the reasons I created the diary is that I really wanted to demonstrate that the Superwoman concept works for anyone.

You just need to be willing to change the way you act and think about the small issues as well as the big ones.

The Superwoman Concept

Before we get into the content of my diary properly, I wanted to remind you of the core elements that I share in *"The Superwoman Lifestyle Blueprint."*

This will serve as a reminder for those who have read the book and as an introduction for those who haven't picked it up yet.

What do you mean you don't have a copy yet?

Please make sure you order a copy right now!

The Superwoman Lifestyle is not some theoretical concept – it's all about using your strengths and making them work in your favor.

It's about thinking long and hard about what is important to you in your life. Most importantly, it's about your thoughts, your priorities and being totally authentic to who you are.

The number one mistake we make as women is comparing ourselves to other women and trying to emulate what we see and admire in them.

Living the Lifestyle

We look at what we see our friends and neighbors doing or perhaps even compare ourselves to our own mothers, trying to measure up.

When you try to take on the life of someone else, you are not living a Superwoman lifestyle.

But here is some good news!

Nine times out of ten, you already have what you need to live the Superwoman lifestyle.

You just need to identify it, unleash it, embrace it and then learn how to work it.

The Superwoman Lifestyle is built on three pillars which I covered in the first book – Business, Beauty and Balance.

• **Business**: A lot of women have great ideas and concepts they can turn into businesses but often they don't step forward with these ideas due to fear, self-doubt and the lack of knowledge on how to pull it all together

• **Beauty**: If you don't feel good about yourself on the inside and the outside, you will be limited in what you can achieve

• **Balance**: Too many women don't push forward with their own dreams because they give too much time to others and neglect themselves

In *"The Superwoman Lifestyle Blueprint"*, I shared a five-step process designed to help you start living the Superwoman Lifestyle right away.

These five steps are:

1) **Begin with your strengths:** Identify and embrace your strengths and your gifts to discover how you can profit from them

2) **Build yourself first:** Invest in your future by making a commitment to your personal growth

3) **Become extraordinary:** Stop believing the excuses that hold you back

4) **Banish fear:** Find your "Fearless Mode" to achieve your full potential

5) **Believe in every opportunity:** Start saying 'yes' today

You'll find the detailed roadmap for achieving that in *"The Superwoman Lifestyle Blueprint."*

Now, let me take you on a journey through my year and share with you the practical reality of living the Superwoman Lifestyle.

I am excited to have you on the journey with me and hope it helps you achieve all the success you deserve.

Vicki Irvin

Visit us at www.SuperWomanLifestyle.com to join thousands of progressive women like yourself and become part of this phenomenal movement that is transforming lives one day at a time.

MONTH 1

Day 1: Mastermind Principle

So here I am in sunny LA sitting poolside at my friend's house in the Valley.

I'm here to attend my Mastermind in LA. It is awesome being in the room with other successful entrepreneurs. We are talking about our successes and our failures, and we are helping each other get to the next level.

Are you familiar with the power of the Mastermind?

Mastermind groups bring together the best and brightest from all industries and together they share what is working and what is not working.

Imagine being coached by 20 ultra-successful people at one time and having them give you ways to tackle your business challenges based on their own experiences.

There is not one big name person I know from ANY industry that does not belong to a Mastermind group and is not being coached and mentored. It is what separates the very successful people from others.

It has most definitely been the reason for my own success and the ROI from being in these elite groups is to the 20th power!

However, I know from all the emails I receive that many women have problems finding mentors or Masterminds to belong to.

Here are a couple of tips...

- Firstly, you want to find mentors, known by other people, who have a history of success.

- Secondly, your mentors should have something you want or are trying to attain. That is what makes you look up to them in the first place.

There is nothing worse than someone pretending to be a "know it all", when, behind the scenes, they have nothing themselves and do not practice what they preach. There are a lot of them out there, so do your homework before you choose someone to be your guide.

Day 2: Today's Thought

If you're not failing every now and again, it's a sign you're not doing anything very innovative.
Woody Allen

Day 3: Making Time for Exercise

While I have been here in LA these past few days, I have been to the gym continuing on with my routine. Just because I go out of town does not mean I use it as a way to slack off on working out.

Gyms are everywhere so I don't give myself any excuses. And when I don't go to the gym, I can still run, walk and do body weight exercise.

I have also continued to eat healthy while allowing myself a cheat day so I don't feel deprived!

Have you found time in your busy schedule to work out? I sure hope so!

Let's face it... we can't be as productive as we want to if we don't feel good. Working out gives us the energy we need to work at maximum capacity and handle all that comes our way.

I urge you to begin thinking about exercise as a normal part of your routine the same way we think about work and eating. It's a mindset and once you get it down, it will be easy for you.

Remember this... besides the physical results we like from working out, the energy levels and health aspects are just as important.

There is no way I would be able to achieve all that I do if I did not work out. I would be too tired and my business would suffer and so would my family life. That's not an option!

So, if you are not exercising regularly, make a commitment now about what you are going to do this week to make it part of your routine.

Day 4: Today's Action

Write a handwritten thank you note to a client or to someone else who has helped you.

Day 5: Juggling Your Family Life

Today it's time to head off back to the East Coast. I have been away from my family for a week here in LA and, while I enjoy the peace and quiet, I miss them.

My son has a loose tooth! He told me his dad took him to the dentist and the x-rays show he has "big boy" teeth coming in. It's definitely early for him to be getting big boy teeth already!

Juggling and balancing family life with work is a challenge, isn't it? And for the moms who are single, I have so much respect for you, too.

A single mom sent me an email last week about her struggles with raising her son alone while running her own business. For a long time she felt so guilty about trying to make money while giving quality time to him as well.

She was writing to thank me for suggesting "chunking" her time. She said she sat down with her son and explained what she was trying to do for him and how she was working hard to give him a better life.

The mom suggested to him that he pick a couple of days out of the week that they can do something together uninterrupted; pure focus time.

She said he picked Tuesdays and Fridays and was so excited about their new schedule. He even started writing down activities and things for them to do.

But the best part was when he gave her a big hug and thanked her for taking such good care of him and working so hard.

I am so happy to hear stories like this! The guilt she was feeling has been lifted by simply carving out set times and explaining to her son why she worked so hard.

Always include your family and keep them informed of your goals and why you are working so hard.

You will find that they will often be your biggest champions and supporters!

Day 8: Today's Thought

Nothing is particularly hard
if you divide it into small jobs.
Henry Ford

Day 9: Managing Your Time

Well now I'm back home and it's time to implement all those great business ideas I picked up at my Mastermind.

Of course, my business kept running successfully while I was away because I've learned how to make the best use of my time.

I often find that allocation of time is one of the biggest problems my coaching clients have in their businesses. Are you making the most of your time or are there areas that need patching up?

As entrepreneurs or small business owners we tend to think that we must do everything ourselves when operating our business.

The main reason is often financial. People often think getting help is too expensive for them.

However, the other reason is falsely believing that nobody can run our business better than us. Does that sound familiar?

I quickly learned early on that I would run myself into the ground if I tried to do every single little thing myself.

Before that, I not only believed that nobody could do it better than me, but I also thought I could handle the accounting and legal aspects as well.

Well needless to say, I woke up quickly!

The first step is determining what your time is even worth.

If you are worth $150 an hour and you are spending time doing data entry into QuickBooks, then you are losing money in your business.

That time could be better spent taking on another client while outsourcing that task to a virtual assistant who charges $15 per hour!

It's all about shifting your mindset and leveraging yourself to maximize productivity that turns into revenue.

You should also be looking at the services you use to ensure you are getting value from them.

Sometimes we have so many things that are automatically debited from our accounts that we forget to take inventory and be sure it's a service or product we still need and use. If it is not, then cancel it.

This is called plugging up the holes in your business so that you continue to increase your flow of money.

So today, I urge you to look at the way you are running your business and identify what holes you can plug.

Day 10: Today's Action

Work out how much an hour of your time is worth – divide the amount you want to earn in a year by the number of hours you want to work. Then, keep that in mind when you decide how to spend every hour.

Day 11: Choosing the Right Media

Today I was doing a phone coaching session with a client who was worried that her advertising wasn't working and was costing her too much money.

Well, we all know that good advertising does work but there are many reasons why advertising can produce disappointing returns. The key is to identify what's wrong or missing.

In this case, I took a look at her ads and they seemed to me to hit all the right buttons, but when I asked her where she was running the ads, it was immediately obvious where the problem was.

She had a fairly expensive upmarket service to offer but was running the ads in budget magazines because they offered the best advertising rates.

With advertising, as in many things, you get what you pay for. You need to have the right media for the message you want to get across and for the market you want to hit.

So I advised her to check out exactly what media her ideal target markets were using and to carefully test some ads there even though it would cost her a bit more.

So today, I want you to take a look at the media you are using to advertise your business – whether you pay for them or not – such as:

- Your website
- Newspaper ads
- Radio ads
- Social media like Facebook and Twitter

Do you know if these media are working for you?

Do you know where your clients and sales are converting from?

As a business owner it is your job to know where every single sale you get is coming from. If you don't track this information, how will you know what is working and what is not?

For example, if you are running an ad in a magazine and also on the radio, you want to know which of them is bringing in more customers.

What if all the sales were coming from the radio, and the newspaper ad wasn't working?

Wouldn't you then want to take the money from the ad that wasn't working and put it into more radio ads that were working?

If you did that then you will have just increased the number of sales you get! But you won't know unless you are tracking very closely.

Further, are you sure the media you use is targeting the right people?

If I had a product geared towards senior citizens, I wouldn't want to try to market to them using online media. Why?

Because market research says that there are still not a lot of seniors who use the internet regularly.

Although the number is growing, it isn't enough for me to spend marketing dollars on that particular media to reach them.

So today, I want you to think about all the media you are using to advertise.

- Do these media match your target market?

- If not, it's time to make some changes!

So get to work Superwoman!

These are critical steps in your business and they are the same steps I used to create my own multi-million dollar business!

Day 12: Today's Thought

Action is the foundational key to all success.
Pablo Picasso

Day 15: Time for the Family

Well it's time now for me to take a break from work and start preparing some dinner.

When I was young growing up in Massachusetts we had a dinner time. Let me tell you, I hated dinner time!

My brother and I were the only kids on the block who had to stop playing and be home at 5pm for dinner. And if we were late, we were in big trouble.

I couldn't understand then why my father was so adamant that we all sit down and eat together, but of course as an adult with my own family I totally get it now.

Reserved family time is a rarity these days. The workforce has changed so much and so has the traditional family unit. But regardless, designated time with family is priceless and is so beneficial.

It's a time to communicate and share your day. It's a time to bond with your family that nobody else can intrude on, and it's a great time to instill values into your children.

Now I must admit that my own family unit looks nothing like when I was a kid growing up. My husband's schedule is one that does not usually bring him home until late evening.

That leaves just my son and me to eat together, but I make sure I use that time to talk about his day at school and to teach him life lessons.

But if you are fortunate enough to have your entire family unit home at the same time, try designating a time that you all sit down and eat together without the TV or any other distractions.

I can honestly say those dinner times helped to shape who I am today and I don't think I turned out so bad!

What steps can you take today to make time for dinner with your family?

Day 16: Today's Action

Walk somewhere instead of driving or taking the elevator.

Day 17: Building a Support Network

Today I attended a fabulous tea party called "Women on Fire" at the Willard Intercontinental hotel in DC.

These tea parties by the beautiful Debbie Phillips are about a lot more than tea. They are a chance for women from all walks of life to come together and share what they are on fire about.

I think the most profound thing that I always walk away with from the Women On Fire events is that, no matter how accomplished you are, we all share similar struggles as women.

We are all trained to put on a happy face and present this well-put-together side of ourselves, even through immense pain, fear and disappointment.

Well we all know that behind closed doors, we ain't that well put together, now are we?

Who knew tea could be so soothing for the soul?

Finding an awesome support system like Women on Fire where we can just be "us" is an important element that I encourage you to connect with.

I have had many women ask me about Women on Fire tea parties. They are held in various cities so check them out and see if there is one close to you.

Otherwise, think about how you can build the kind of support network that is going to help you.

Day 18: Today's Thought

I honestly think it is better to be a failure at something you love than to be a success at something you hate.
George Burns

Day 19: Reviewing Your Website

I've been spending some time today with my web guy making a few tweaks to my site.

I'm getting good results with my site but there are always changes we can make based on analyzing the response we are getting and seeing what works well.

So based on my experience, I'm going to ask you to take a look at your website today.

- Do you have a website for your business that is generating income?

Or

- Do you have what I call an online business card?

I find that many small business owners and entrepreneurs are not clear on what the purpose of a website is.

The majority of people believe it is a place to tell people to go and check out what their company, business or service is all about… and then hope they give you a call and want to buy from you.

To take it a step further, people believe the flashier their website is, with awesome graphics and music, that they will have a real edge up on their competition.

Not so; those are not the things that turn your website into a cash generating machine.

The purpose of your website should be to capture a prospect's name and email so that you can continue to market to them.

This is done by using an opt-in box. In order for someone to actually give you this information, you need to offer them something in exchange such as a free report or CD about your product.

This is called lead generation.

At the point a prospect gives you their name and email they have just become a lead. It is then your job to communicate with that lead about your services and establish a relationship with them so that they get to know you.

Rarely do people buy from you the first time; it takes multiple communications before most are ready to actually buy.

For this reason alone, not having an opt-in box and a way to communicate with prospects is leaving thousands and thousands of dollars on the table.

So what do you have? A lead-generating website or just an online business card stuck out there in cyberspace?

If your site is not generating leads, what can you do today to make it start working harder for you?

Day 22: Today's Action
Make sure you drink at least a liter of water.

Day 23: Feeling Good About Your Body
So I've just come back from a trip to the gym where I've spent some time working out and now I'm energized to get on with some work.

I enjoy going to the gym and make it part of my routine but if the gym doesn't work for you, that's no excuse to miss out on exercise.

You don't have to go to the gym to get a good workout in. If you are pressed for time, you can always invest in a few pieces of equipment from a sporting goods store.

I have a physio-ball, a resistance band and various dumbbells. I transformed my entire body using those things and eating right. I worked out in my living room and saw instant results!

I am the type of person who likes to switch it up from time to time to keep myself motivated. In good weather, I like to run outside or go to a track. There are just so many things you can do to get healthy.

As women we are not able to perform to our maximum level if we do not feel good about our bodies and health. It hinders us from doing a lot of things and keeps us out of balance.

I can guarantee you that if you start to do things for your health and fitness, it will give you results and you will prosper in all areas of your life.

That synergy has to be there, it is just how we are built. But sometimes we need a little extra motivation to make us do things.

A great motivator for getting fit can be simply writing down some reasons why you want to be fit.

Why not try that now? Write down three benefits of improving your fitness and then take some action.

Day 24: Today's Thought

If you can dream it, you can do it.
Walt Disney

Day 25: Internet Marketing

Last night I conducted a Superwoman Lifestyle coaching meeting.

Fabulous women business owners, entrepreneurs, and those aspiring to be came out to learn strategies on how to market their business both online and offline.

Internet marketing is something my husband and I have been into for years and other people are catching on that internet marketing is something everyone should learn.

Collectively we have marketed a wide range of businesses online using internet marketing strategies. I get tons of email from women wanting to break into this area and I am glad to see such an interest.

However, many people are confused as to exactly what internet marketing is and how it works.

First, let me make it clear that there are VERY few businesses that cannot be marketed online.

So, no matter what your business is – and how much money you are making using the marketing strategies you currently have – if you are not marketing online, you are leaving thousands and thousands of dollars on the table that could be in your bank account.

Previously, I mentioned the importance of having an opt-in box on your website to capture names and email addresses but it goes deeper than that.

Your first job is to build up your list of prospects. You need to offer something free in exchange for your prospect's name and email such as:
- CD
- DVD

- E-book
- Report

These are all called "widgets." Your widget should be something of value that would benefit your prospects so that they want it enough to give you their contact information.

When you get people to give you their contact information, you can turn those leads in customers by continuously communicating with them.

So what widget can you offer to encourage people to give you their details – or what can you do to make your current widget better?

Day 26: Today's Action

Take at least one new action that will help get
you a new client or customer.

Day 29: Social Marketing

I've just made a quick post on my Facebook page and I must say it's a great way of reaching out to new people and staying in touch.

Are you using social marketing in your business at all – such as Facebook or Twitter? And if you are using social marketing, are you using it effectively?

I recently spoke to a social media specialist and told them how I was using it in my business. Turns out I am using it the right way, which was great to know. But we also talked about how people are NOT using it correctly.

Social media should be used to generate business or clients. It is okay to infuse personality into your social marketing, but it is not okay to get too personal or share stuff that will turn off your audience.

In addition, it is easy to become addicted to social media and waste time doing things that do not generate income. So if you are using social media, be honest with yourself and assess if you are making money from it, or just staying busy.

Another big mistake is solely relying on social media from which to build a business. It should be used as a supplement to your marketing, not a sole source.

If you are using it as a sole source, that is probably the reason you are not getting the results you want. You do not ever want to rely on just one leg of marketing to build or support your business; doing so will leave you vulnerable.

Try to limit the time you spend on social media sites. You should develop a formula of spending about 1 hour per day on your social media marketing.

Anything more means you are probably addicted and probably not doing things that are income generating.

I must admit that I love social media and I love the fun aspects of it as well. But when it comes to building my business, I try to stay focused and condense my time to one hour.

You must also be sure you are measuring the results you are getting from these sites. If you don't have a way of knowing whether what you are doing is working, then you are making a huge mistake.

So take inventory of your social media marketing and make the necessary tweaks to ensure you are monetizing it!

Day 30: Today's Thought

Success doesn't come to you... you go to it.
Marva Collins

Looking Back and Looking Forward

What are the top five things you have learned this month?

1.

2.

3.

4.

5.

What are the top five actions you will take next month?

1.

2.

3.

4.

5.

MONTH 2

Day 1: Talking About What You Do

My husband and I hosted our monthly marketing meeting last night.

Each month people travel near and far to hear us talk about marketing strategies and how to get more clients. Last night we talked about a unique technique on how to use blogs.

The people who were there couldn't wait to get home and implement what we gave out into their own businesses. I'll have more to say about blogs another day but today I want to get back to the basics.

I find that most people cannot tell you what they do in 30 seconds or less. If you are an entrepreneur, you should be able to clearly and concisely tell anyone what you do very quickly. Sounds simple, right? Well it's not.

You may know what it is that you do conceptually, but do you know how to translate that into a quick spiel that will capture the attention of the person inquiring? And I don't mean using fancy words that they may not even understand.

31

I am referring to statements that are attention grabbers and pique the interest of the person. Something that makes them say, "Wow, tell me more."

You only have a few seconds to captivate the attention of a prospect whether it is in person, on your website, or any other form of advertising you use. So what you say has to be clear and interesting.

I'll give you an example. I worked with a young lady last night at my meeting on this very exercise. She is in the field of performance improvement and her target market is business owners.

She has the expertise of evaluating employees using various tools to measure performance on the job. Although that is exactly what she does, it isn't clear to someone who is not in that field.

If she was to be at an event talking to the CEO of a company trying to sell her service to them, that spiel would probably not grab their attention.

BUT, if she said something like, *"I specialize in showing small business owners how they are losing thousands and thousands of dollars each month through poor employee training and hiring and how they can recover that money in 90 days."*

Now THAT would grab my attention if I was a CEO. Everyone wants to know how to recoup lost money or avoid losing money. At that point, the CEO would probably want to learn more right away!

This task sounds simple, but I challenge you to try it. You will probably find you need to practice and refine it.

Try out what you come up with on friends or family and gauge the reactions you get. Test, test, test. Once you find a statement that is a winner, you are on your way!

Day 2: Today's Thought

Never mistake activity for achievement.
John Wooden

Day 3: We All Have Choices

I have been speaking for a lot of organizations and events the last few weekends, and meeting some amazing people! Many of my presentations have been on my first book *"The Superwoman Lifestyle Blueprint"* and I am thrilled the message has resonated with so many women. That has been my goal all along.

If you haven't picked up your copy yet, this is a must read if I may say so myself!

Someone asked me the other day how I get so much done. They told me that I must not have a problem in the world. Ummm yeah, right, I WISH!

Let' get down and dirty for a minute. EVERYONE has problems. Life is not a bed of roses for anyone 365 days of the year. I have LOTS of problems and I have faced MANY challenges.

I lost a baby at 8 months of pregnancy and had to deliver a stillborn. My house was invaded a couple of years ago and my family was held at gunpoint by now convicted serial killers who committed multiple murders.

Not to mention the everyday problems of raising my son, having a marriage and everything else life brings your way. I have made money, but I have lost LOTS of money, too.

But here is what I have learned. You can either let circumstances make you, or break you. Whining, complaining and moaning about how unfair life is gets you nowhere!

People go through divorces; we lose parents, children and loved ones. We lose money. We lose jobs, we lose houses. But we HAVE to be resilient!! We can't roll over and be defeated!

Here is what helps me when I feel myself sinking... I realize that I am not alone. I am not the only one who has faced a challenge. There is nothing unique about my circumstances. It's called life.

To help out, I surround myself with positive like-minded people who can push me:

- REAL people who tell the truth and don't pretend to be perfect.
- People who share their own stories of bad times, and show you how they made it through.

What I DON'T do is call up the drama queens and kings who LOVE misery. They LOVE to hear your stories because they live in a constant state of chaos and even thrive on it.

These people don't help you to see the light on the other side. Instead, they talk to you about how life is so unfair and how the both of you have been handed a bad card. These are the excuse makers who blame everyone else but themselves for their situations.

These are the people who believe others owe them something. Know anybody like this?

I have clients who are battling cancer, divorce and a myriad of other problems. But guess what? They are some of the most positive upbeat people I have ever met in my life who are determined to make it through.

Time heals everything; each day it gets better and better! And when you surround yourself with other people to help push you, you can't lose.

So if you are feeling down and out today, look for the positive and know that your day is coming as long as you make the decision to rise above it, rather than wallow in it. After all, we all have choices!

Day 4: Today's Action

Clear out your closets and make space for something new in your life.

Day 5: Needs and Wants

Today I was having a long chat with a client who has so much to offer in what she does but she was feeling pretty down about her business.

She was feeling frustrated and had that sense that she wasn't getting her message through to her prospects.

We were chatting and she came out with that phrase that I hear so often, *"I know they need what I am offering but I can't seem to convince enough people."*

Whenever I hear that I know it's time to back up and think differently.

Think about this... people will never stop spending money on the things they want. Do you notice I said WANT and not NEED?

As a business owner or entrepreneur, it is your responsibility to give your target audience what they want.

People make buying decisions based on wants. How many times have you allowed things you NEED to suffer because you WANTED something else?

You may need to pay your gas bill, but when it comes down to that new pair of designer shoes that you want, what will the final decision be? Get my point?

So do not design your marketing strategy around your personal perception of what your clients need.

You will not make it doing that. It is your job to talk to them and see what they WANT. Sounds simple, but it's a big mistake many people make.

So you need to find out what your customers and prospects want and then talk to them about how what you offer will help them get it.

That will make a big difference in how you feel and will make your customers happier, too!

Day 8: Today's Thought

It's never too late to be what you might have been.
George Eliot

Day 9: Balancing Work and Life

I've been reading my mentor's magazine and she gave some great advice on work-life balance.

She validated what I've said previously many times... that you have to find the balance in your life that works for YOU without making you insane.

What works for one Superwoman may not work for another.

Don't try to be exactly like someone else, find your own rhythm. And for goodness sake STOP FEELING GUILTY.

Let's face it; no matter how hard we try we cannot be everything to everybody. It is okay. It is impossible.

All we can do is our very best and, at the end of the day, know we gave it our all.

Anyone expecting more than that from you can GO FLY A KITE! Say it with me... GO FLY A KITE!

Day 10: Today's Action

Make a list of all your outstanding tasks and prioritize them.

Day 11: The Power of Feedback

I'm hosting a big event in a couple of days and I am excited! I have women flying in from Texas, Florida, and Georgia to name a few!

We are running around finalizing details today and tomorrow I am off to the hair salon and shopping so I can look my best; we are being filmed!

Superwoman Lifestyle is sponsoring this all women's event. I am working on my next women's retreat already, but this one will be for all the women business owners and entrepreneurs who are seeking ways to increase their client base and explode their income.

Women are struggling to keep their businesses afloat and it is because they lack the marketing knowledge. I have been coaching women on how to learn and employ the same strategies that I use for all my businesses that keep my events jam-packed with no shortage of clients in ANY economy.

The main thing is you have to invest in educating yourself! I gladly pay to belong to Mastermind groups of the most successful people and it pays off BIG TIME!

Talking of Mastermind groups, my husband is at one of his groups this week. He attends with many of the top internet marketers in the world.

I know that when I attend these Masterminds with my husband, I walk away with the latest and greatest strategies in the industry.

These guys are so forthcoming with their knowledge and are always very helpful.

The same thing applies when I attend my own Mastermind with Ali Brown; she too is a wealth of knowledge and always goes above and beyond to assist.

Day 12: Today's Thought

Shoot for the moon. Even if you miss, you will land amongst the stars.
Les Brown

Day 15: The Value of Education

I mentioned the other day that my husband was away at one of his Masterminds.

He presented a project I am working on for critique. Long story short, they ripped me up big time!

But I recognize the criticism is constructive and – no matter how brutal – it is designed to give me vital improvements that will impact my bottom line in a big way.

You see – one change to your website or sales letter can increase your conversion by thousands of dollars.

That is why studying and becoming an avid student of marketing is what can change your whole business life, regardless of what industry you are in!

Knowing the value of education and investing in yourself is what makes you successful.

As I am typing this, I just received an email from a real estate investing student of mine.

She has increased her net worth by $500,000 since coming through my real estate investing training, and just flipped a property and netted about $45,000 for her bank account.

When I think about the type of woman she is, she is front and center at all of our ongoing trainings and stays connected to our group. She sees the value in educating and investing in herself. Once you have that mindset down, the tides will turn in your favor.

Day 16: Today's Action

Change one thing about the email opt-in box on your website – such as the headline, the font or the graphic – and see what difference it makes to your opt-in rate.

Day 17: Warped View of Your Body

Are you suffering from a warped view of your own body image? I know I go through this weekly myself. I work hard in the gym, but sometimes I don't see what I want to see in the mirror.

We hold ourselves to such high standards that it is easy to miss the small changes and improvements we have made. It's so much easier for other people to see your progress. How many times do you get paid a compliment or someone asks if you lost weight? You kind of look at them like, "Me?" Yes you!

When you are constantly stepping on the scale or looking at your rear from every angle possible, it's easy not to see progress and miss the changes. Here is a quick remedy for that – take 'before' and 'after' pictures of yourself.

Pictures do not lie and you will have documentation of your hard work. When you can see your progress it serves as a motivator to keep working hard. Everyone needs motivation for fitness and it sure is nice when people notice, it feels great!

Day 18: Today's Thought

*Being defeated is often a temporary condition. Giving up
is what makes it permanent.*
Marilyn vos Savant

Day 19: Big List Building Mistake

Someone asked me today if it was okay to build their prospect list by just adding people's names to their contacts in their email.

The answer is NO! As a professional you have got to allow people to opt into what you are offering on their own. Nothing makes me crazier than for someone to just put my email on their list and start blasting me with their promotions.

First, I am resentful I have been illegally added to their list (and yes, there are entities that monitor this... it's called SPAM).

Second, even if they had a great product or service I am already turned off by the fact they do not know the proper way to build a list and added me without my permission. So much so that I will not deal with them and demand to be removed.

Think about it... why blast people with your product promotion when you do not even know if they are interested in what you are selling or offering? That is not a prospect list; that is an "I hope they are into what I have" list and it's like marketing sand to the desert.

Marketing is about finding qualified people interested in what you do, not hoping and wishing. That is a waste of time, energy and money... and did I mention it's SPAM? Nobody wants to be spammed, trust me I know.

When I was marketing an event I was holding for real estate, my contact database system mistakenly sent my emails to my husband's martial arts list.

Well, I was called every name in the book by people who received that email. Why?

Because they are interested in martial arts not real estate and they did not know who I was. This is a perfect example of why you have to allow people to give you permission to market to them.

Moral of the story? Invest in a contact management system that allows your prospects to opt into what you are offering.

It is the legal and ethical way and it is the ONLY way to build a list of qualified leads that you can turn into raving fans!

Day 22: Today's Action

If you're struggling with your exercise routine, find a different way to exercise such as taking up a new hobby.

Day 23: Are You Serious?

I spoke this past weekend at the Greater Washington Court Reporters Association and had a great time helping them discover other streams of income within their existing business!

But I missed my Millionaire Protégé Club Meeting in LA as a result. I heard it was awesome as usual. I also missed a chance to travel to Spain with my husband. If only I could split myself into three people!

As a Superwoman, I'm sure you wish you had the power to clone yourself as well!

So today I want to talk about how serious you are about your business.

I hear people all the time say they wish to be an entrepreneur and that they don't want to work for anyone else. But I am not so sure everyone understands how hard you have to work in order to have a business that generates income and continues to grow.

It doesn't normally happen overnight and it certainly doesn't happen without you busting your behind.

I can usually tell the people who will be successful in business versus those who will struggle. There tend to be common success traits that entrepreneurs will possess.

One is the willingness to learn any and everything they can by reading, listening to educational CDs, investing in a coaching program and devouring everything they can.

Next is the person who actually takes action on what they learn and puts it to use. One of the things you cannot expect someone else to do is to take your business seriously when they see you don't.

I have fired clients who were not serious because they expected me to do everything for them. If you don't have the desire to do what needs to be done in your own business, you certainly can't expect anyone else to rise to the occasion for you.

A successful entrepreneur will work on things in their business every single day. They will give up the things they enjoy in order to sacrifice while they are getting things going. The person who would rather spend their time on things that are "fun" but don't pertain to them growing their business is the person who is not in it for the long haul.

If you don't have a clear vision for your business, it is time to write down your goals. The most successful people in the world write down their goals and revisit them often. How will you get anywhere without a road map?

There have to be points of arrival along the way to your ultimate goal and it is your job to map out how to reach each milestone that will catapult you closer and closer.

With no goals, you have no real plan. In fact you are operating like a fish out of water. I have been there, done that.

It leaves you frustrated and ready to give up. But once you come up with a real and attainable plan, you immediately have to have something to work with and refer back to.

Remember that goals have to be revisited and revamped from time to time due to all types of changes and that is normal and perfectly fine.

So for the entrepreneur who is serious, this is your path. It starts with changing your mindset and priorities. So what's it going to be? Are you serious or not?

Day 24: Today's Thought
You always pass failure on the way to success.
Mickey Rooney

Day 25: Taking the First Step

I was able to take some time and relax on my boat earlier this week. My husband Lloyd had just got back in town from the Jiu-Jitsu world championships and he came back with a whole lot of gold medals for his team which means they had a great year and made some history.

We decided to call up some friends and hit the water and what an awesome time we had. Of course the conversation on the boat turned to marketing, but that's great because we all continue to learn the latest and greatest cutting edge strategies... which means I can pass them on to you!

But let me start with a question.

If I were to do a search and try to find out something about you online, would anything come up? If not, you have no presence on the internet and that is a fatal mistake. Do you know that you can create a huge buzz about yourself or your business, product or service by writing on various blogs?

The blogs you write end up getting "indexed" and appear when people do searches on Google or Yahoo. Let me repeat myself here... you can do that at no cost and most people don't know how. It's one of the easiest things you can do to position yourself as an expert in your field.

You do this by using "keywords" in your writing that are specific to what you do. For example, if I had a jewelry company or product I wanted to promote in the MD area, I would use keywords throughout my blog post that would show up under "jewelry in MD" so that when people out there were looking for a jewelry company, I would appear in those search engine results.

It is a very simple process to maintain and write a blog. You create a way to market yourself or business that costs you zero dollars.

So my little assignment for you is to go to Google and put in your name or business name.

If nothing about you appears in the search results, you are lost in cyberspace and it is time to create your presence on the internet. I am giving you a way to do this that costs you nothing!

There are many more ways of doing this that cost you nothing, but one of the best ways to get started is with a blog.

You can set yourself up with a free WordPress blog and start writing content on your product or service to position yourself as an expert.

This is a great way to get started blogging, so check it out and start creating a buzz about yourself! It's one of the best things you can do for your business.

Day 26: Today's Action

Identify someone who reaches the same market as you – but is not a competitor – and contact them to discuss how you can work together for mutual benefit.

Day 29: Shock Yourself Into Action

My next Mastermind meeting with my Platinum coaching students is coming up in a few days. Three times per year we get together in a room for two days and tackle business challenges, strategies and ideas.

Most importantly, the group provides suggestions, feedback and priceless insight to help each member accelerate their business as quickly as possible.

In a nutshell, the Mastermind is a serious kick in the butt! It's structured to force business owners to take fast action and be accountable, something we ALL need! Trying to figure out your business on your own doesn't work, plain and simple.

Women are in charge of their kids, their households, the bills, the school functions, homework, and everything else we do on a daily basis.

- We hold our kids accountable for good behavior, good manners, and good grades.
- We keep our husbands on track and let them think they are in charge when we know, without us, there would be chaos!

But who holds US accountable for doing what we need to do to realize our goals and aspirations? Usually we have nobody.

- Friends who don't get the entrepreneurial desire and lifestyle tell us we are crazy.
- Family normally tells us we are crazy for even trying and encourages us to stop dreaming.

Not to mention the negative people who tear you down regularly for daring to be extraordinary and wanting something more for yourself.

Sound familiar? Battling all of those forces by yourself is almost impossible. Even the most driven and self-motivated person you know can't fight all of that 24/7.

It's easy to let yourself off the hook and make up excuses as to why you can't do this or why you can't do that. Why this isn't working and how you just don't have enough hours in the day. Why someone else can make it work, but you just can't catch a break.

But at the end of the day, they are just excuses – our immediate defense mechanism when we want an easy way out because we become overwhelmed and can't imagine ourselves really making it.

That is why having someone else to hold you accountable is the key to you consistently moving forward and making big leaps in your business and life.

I wish I could say I get so much done because I wake up every day giving it my 100%, but I would be lying. The truth is that I get so much done because I have people holding me accountable and because I invest in myself. Without that single factor I would be making excuses and letting myself off the hook.

Do you have that? Do you have a person holding your feet to the fire? If not, you have to get that and get it QUICK!

Day 30: Today's Thought

Great things are not done by impulse, but by a series of small things brought together.
Vincent Van Gogh

Looking Back and Looking Forward

What are the top five things you have learned this month?

1.

2.

3.

4.

5.

What are the top five actions you will take next month?

1.

2.

3.

4.

5.

MONTH 3

Day 1: Sharing Yourself

I just got back in town yesterday from a GREAT anniversary vacation that my husband Lloyd surprised me with. He invited some of our good friends who popped up in the airport and shocked me. I had no clue they were coming.

We had a great time in Miami with the kids, relaxing by the pool most of the time. Group family vacations are a great time when you are in good company!

But I am back and ready for business today and I want to know how you are communicating with your list? How often? What are you saying and what great content are you giving out?

If you have a list of prospects and customers, they should always know that you are there and never forget about you. If you allow them to forget you are there, then you probably lost a sale.

Do your customers know anything about you? If not, they should.

It is very important to infuse personality into your communications with your list. Research shows that people do business with people they like and can relate to. How often have you shopped around for something and made your final decision based on how the person made you feel? You do it all the time without even thinking about it... and that is how you should think about your customer base.

It is perfectly fine to tell things and stories about yourself and life to your clients. It makes you seem human and touchable and people like that. So whether you have a blog you write on, an ezine you send to your list, or whatever way you communicate, my challenge to you is for you to start revealing a more personal side of yourself and letting your customers and clients get to know you.

In addition, you should be communicating at least once per week, but probably even more. You should also be giving out great content and useful information that someone can actually take and use. If you are providing your audience great content and they unsubscribe from your list, then they probably aren't the target client you are looking for anyway. Remember, you are only interested in communicating with someone interested in your services.

So this week, look at your communication frequency, what your message is, how you are saying it, and whether or not you have any personality in your writings. Tweaking these things will boost your sales immediately!

Day 2: Today's Thought

When I thought I couldn't go on, I forced myself to keep going. My success is based on persistence, not luck.
Estee Lauder

Day 3: Eating Right

As I mentioned, I was in Miami for a few days. It is so easy to get sidelined with healthy eating and exercise when you are out of town. However, it is even easier to stay on track these days.

Hotels serve healthy meals and so do the nearby restaurants. And of course hotels have gyms. I did pretty well by ordering egg white omelets and eating oatmeal for breakfast.

I allowed myself one cheat meal per day. And I got up early in the morning to hit the gym so that I wouldn't take any time away from my vacation. Doing that allows you to not feel that guilt. The key to healthy living is balance. You don't have to kill yourself every day, but you should dedicate time to making sure that you take care of your health by eating right and getting your blood pumping.

Day 4: Today's Action

A Superwoman like yourself often gets caught up in nurturing everyone else and not taking time for herself and we can't have that. Gather a group of your friends together, set a date and go nurture yourself for a few hours. You will feel better instantly!

Day 5: Finding Time for What Matters

When you feel burned out and tired, it is hard to give attention to the things that matter the most in your life.

If you are like me, finding time to do everything in your life and do it well is a big challenge. Is your family suffering as a result of you being pulled in so many different directions?

Let's look at your relationship with your spouse or significant other.

Have you carved out any special time to nurture your relationship?

How about a date night? Yes, couples who have been together a long time still need to date. Relationships are work and the work doesn't stop once you walk down the aisle.

You cannot be productive in your business if your personal relationships are suffering.

As women, we tend to shut down when things in our life are out of balance. That is why your goal as a Superwoman is to work on all areas of your life so that you remain productive and fulfilled.

So take a look at what relationships have been suffering. It is no fun making it to the top if you are alone when you get there!

Day 8: Today's Thought

I feel that luck is preparation meeting opportunity.
Oprah Winfrey

Day 9: Expanding Into New Areas

I have just come off a live 4-day event with my husband Lloyd. He had over 270 business owners fly in from all over the world including China and Australia to come and learn effective marketing strategies.

I presented for them on branding and marketing messages to make you stand out and attract more clients and opportunity. It was an amazing crowd and more came out of it than I expected!

Speaking of live events, just how are you profiting in your business? Are you making money from more than one aspect of your business?

- Are you doing live events?
- Are you speaking?
- Are you conducting teleseminars?
- Do you have a coaching program?

From my experience, most entrepreneurs could and should be profiting from all of the above. You never want to stay so narrowly-focused in your business to the point you are stepping over thousands and thousands of dollars by not expanding the scope of what you are doing.

The worst number in business in "1" because if that "1" income stream ever goes away, so will your business. That is why you must proactively create multiple profit centers within your core business to arm you against that. Bullet-proof your business!

If you have never considered expanding the scope of your business, then today I want you to seriously think about it. Yes, there is a proper way of doing live events, creating talks, and creating profitable coaching programs.

As with anything, you have to invest in learning how to get the knowledge to do so.

Day 10: Today's Action

Increase your prices by 20% and see how it affects your sales (you'll probably find the impact is less than you expect).

Day 11: Overcoming Overwhelm

I am having a personal crisis today! I am about to leave town and all of the fish I prepared will be left in my refrigerator to go bad!

As you probably know by now, I am a stickler for eating right and eating five meals each day. I am such a die-hard that I pack up meals and take them to the strangest places with me.

Women are always curious to know what I am eating. I stick with fish and chicken, some kind of green veggie and a good carb like brown whole grain rice, sweet potatoes or Ezekiel bread.

I eat egg whites and oatmeal for breakfast just about every day. Although this may sound too much like a routine for you, I made it a habit.

It takes 21 days to make or break a habit. Once I settled into this routine, it became a way of life. That doesn't mean I can't indulge and splurge every now and then because I can.

But I have vowed to live a healthy lifestyle and that habit is now with me.

There is nothing special about how I eat. You can do the same thing with the same discipline.

The benefits are huge motivators. Being able to fit into my clothes, having energy and knowing that it's good for my overall health is what keeps me going.

Here is an example of a typical day for me. I took my son to school, worked on an internet marketing project, worked out, ate all five of my healthy meals that I prepared in advance, conducted a Superwoman Lifestyle meeting until about 9:00pm, came home and packed for a business trip.

So trust me when I say I understand how hard it is to stay balanced, focused and cater to friends, family and kids! Sometimes it is downright overwhelming.

So, here's a tip. When you feel overwhelmed, take a moment to breathe and relax.

You can only do but so much. Make a list of what is most important and tackle those things first. If you have made a promise to one of your kids, follow through.

If you made a date with your spouse or significant other, follow through.

Put everything else on the back burner and honor your family commitments. Then go back to everything else.

Being a Superwoman gives you the right to hang up your cape every now and then!

So make a list of what's most important in your life today and make sure you make these points your top priority.

Day 12: Today's Thought

Remembering you are going to die is the best way I know to avoid the trap of thinking you have something to lose. You are already naked. There is no reason not to follow your heart.
Steve Jobs

Day 15: My Mentor's Top Tips

I was in LA last weekend at my mentor James Malinchak's four-day live event. There were over 600 of us there and the networking and information were priceless!

I was SUPER happy to see a couple of my Superwoman Platinum Mastermind members and some coaching clients in attendance; I was able to connect them with some amazing people.

My husband Lloyd also had a bunch of his Mastermind members there as well, so it was a GREAT time!

If you weren't at the event, this is your lucky day! I want to share just a FEW of the money-making tips and information nuggets I walked away with and I hope you put it to use too! These are million dollar tips from James, so TAKE NOTES!!!

- Stop taking advice from people who have not experienced success in their own business, many of these people love to give advice although they just can't seem to make it happen for themselves... hmmmmm.

- NEVER turn off your marketing machine; the minute you stop marketing, your business will go waaayyyyy down.

- Don't fill your ego, fill your bank account. Too many people are caught up in getting accolades from others; but if the people telling you how great you are aren't BUYING from you, then something is not working. Don't get caught in the hype, figure out how to make money!

- If you are running a business, then treat it like a business. The minute you devalue yourself or your products and services is the minute others will devalue you as well.

- Don't try to take on a million tasks at once, work on one big thing and see it through to completion. It will motivate you to tackle the next one and, before you know it, you will have more done in a month than you did in six months!

- Entrepreneurs need products we can sell; stay in a mode of product creation so that you always have fresh content to share with your subscribers.

- SPIDER WEBBING: The act of spreading as much of your content as possible in as many places as possible so that you are constantly bringing new prospects into your funnel. Be everywhere!

I literally have pages and pages of notes and I am already implementing them into my own business! The key to success is self-investment and plugging into people who can elevate your income in the quickest amount of time.

That's why every single successful person you see and admire has a coach or mentor. Nobody can do it alone!

Day 16: Today's Action

Make a change in your appearance – new clothes or new hairstyle.

Day 17: Tweaking Your Routine

Okay, is this you? Do you want to work out, but you can't visualize the results or think it will just take too long to reach your goal so you don't bother?

I know that I can be impatient when I want to achieve a goal and I want results like... yesterday.

So I have to mentally prepare myself to have patience and realize the most important thing is just getting started. And when I see minor changes it pushes me even further.

Today, I want you to do something – anything that switches up your routine as it pertains to fitness. Stop eating red meat for a month and stick to fish; watch how quickly you see those results!

If you have been walking on the treadmill, up your pace/speed and incline and watch how you see those results.

If you are lifting weights, instead of reaching for 15lb weights, grab the 20s for your next set.

Just like in business, you have always got to push yourself to greater heights. Minor tweaks in your routine make all the difference in the world!

Day 18: Today's Thought

Either you run the day or the day runs you.
Jim Rohn

Day 19: Eating Right

I have been working from my husband's martial arts school the past week and watching the grueling training schedule the guys who fight have to go through.

These guys train up to three times per day, stay on strict meal plans and work out like crazy… and many of them have full time jobs. When I see that kind of discipline and drive, it makes what I have to do to stay in shape pale in comparison.

It seems many women have the same challenges. I am going to give you a tip. The meal plan that you stay on is what makes all the difference in the world.

There truly is no point in working out if you blow all the hard work you put in by eating things that are unhealthy.

Notice that I did not say diet, I said meal plan. I have never been on a diet in my life; instead the goal is to adopt a healthy meal plan and way of living that becomes a routine. When I go to the grocery store I do not buy things that are unhealthy and bring them into my house.

That is the first step in removing all temptation. When I have to eat out, there are usually healthy choices in all restaurants these days.

Eating a well-balanced meal plan makes you feel better and have sustained energy. Eating small meals every 2-3 hours keeps your metabolism burning fat all day.

I currently eat five small meals each day and I am never hungry. I only drink water and stay away from soda and juices that are loaded with extra empty calories.

Don't overwhelm yourself on the quest to live a healthier lifestyle. Make small adjustments and changes and gradually add in bigger steps.

I guarantee that any small step you take will immediately yield you positive results. And once you see that happening, you will be motivated to take the next step!

Day 22: Today's Action

Conduct a survey of your customers to find their top questions then create answers to these questions and turn it into a product that you can sell or give away as a widget to build your list.

Day 23: Taking a Break

I have been working non-stop! Today, I decided to take a breather.

I'm off to the gym to work out with my father-in-law and then I am going to do a whole bunch of NOTHING.

I have some major real estate projects that are about to take the area by storm and my whirlwind will be starting up again. That is why I am taking some time to just relax.

As women we think we have to keep on moving non-stop because that is what we are used to. But we are allowed to take time for ourselves... guilt free!

Give yourself credit for all you do, remember you are human and enjoy all your accomplishments no matter how big or small. Otherwise life will just pass you by!

Day 24: Today's Thought

What you do today can improve all your tomorrows.
Ralph Marston

Day 25: Selling Secrets

I received an email from a woman who is excited to be launching her own business, but petrified about having to sell and market herself.

Sales and marketing remains one of the top roadblocks for entrepreneurs, it makes people so uncomfortable! I get it, I really do. Selling has a negative connotation to it due to all those unscrupulous and unethical people portrayed on TV.

But when you believe in what you do, and you believe you have something great to share with the world, it truly is your job as an entrepreneur to get the word out to the universe about what you have to offer.

The more people who know about you, the more people you will be able to help and affect change. Listen, if you don't exude confidence in what you do, how can you expect someone else to believe in you?

People want to see that YOU believe in yourself before they will even think about taking a chance on you.

Sales and marketing don't have to be hard when you change your mindset on how you approach the process. Knowing your target market, knowing your ideal client and all their hot buttons, helps you to deliver the right message that really hits home with them.

Your message will be clear, the benefits apparent and your delivery will be perfect and filled with the winning confidence that prospects want to see.

If you don't believe sales and marketing strategies are a must have, then you are going to have a rough road ahead of you. It doesn't matter how great your product or service is, your business will not flourish until you learn the RIGHT way of:

- Attracting a prospect
- Building rapport with a prospect
- Converting a prospect to a client
- Then retaining your client so they become a customer for life.

Day 26: Today's Action

List people who suck up your energy and work out how to get them out of your life.

Day 29: Speaking for Profit

I'm on my way to San Antonio, Texas today where I have the honor of speaking at and opening up a major event for women entrepreneurs.

They are looking to learn from some of the sharpest women out there... women who have built multi-million dollar businesses by mastering business systems and marketing.

I am going to share my philosophies on living a Superwoman Lifestyle and how self-investment is the secret weapon to success. I am so pumped up!

Have you thought about being a speaker before? It's amazing how many women I work with who are coaches or consultants, but have a burning desire to get on stage and speak, too. And you know what I say to that? AWESOME!

If you have an expertise and message that others could benefit from, by all means, you too should become a speaker. With so many people having events, the need for good qualified speakers is in high demand.

As an entrepreneur you should always be looking for other ways to profit from your core business. Sure, I could just be a coach, but why would I want to do that? I can also get on other people's stages and deliver great content to their audience while being paid to do so.

In turn, that also helps to grow my own list or following because most of the people you speak in front of will end up joining up and connecting with you to learn even more.

Speaking is one of the BEST ways to get your message out to the world while allowing people an amazing chance to get to know all about you. Connection is key and the single best place to connect is live and in person. Nothing tops that.

Please don't allow fear of speaking to prevent you from pursuing your message either!

I know that speaking is one of the most feared things in the world for people, but when you work with someone to develop a great signature "talk" that you know is going to rock the house, your confidence level will go up!

Day 30: Today's Thought

Do you want to know who you are? Don't ask. Act!
Action will delineate and define you.
Thomas Jefferson

Looking Back and Looking Forward

What are the top five things you have learned this month?

1.

2.

3.

4.

5.

What are the top five actions you will take next month?

1.

2.

3.

4.

5.

MONTH 4

Day 1: Are You Tooting Your Horn?

On my way to San Antonio, I ended up stuck in the airport overnight! I had to be on a live set the next morning ready to go and representing for the ladies.

I pulled it together, but I was so tired I had to keep moving in order to prevent myself from falling asleep! Mission accomplished, thank goodness!

Next weekend I am speaking at an internet marketing event in DC and, of course, once again I am the only woman!

There is a lack of good female speakers out there, so make sure you capitalize on that opportunity, the market is wide open! I always encourage my clients to add speaking to their income streams!

Oh, and I did an interview for the cover of a new magazine yesterday, and I am excited about that!

Working hard doesn't necessarily mean you are accomplishing anything. If you spend all of your time spinning in circles with no REAL profit or growth to show for it, then you are wasting your time.

If what you are doing it not working, then why do you keep on doing it? It's obvious to the trained eye when someone is really profiting in their business and when they are not. A person going through the motions is on to something new every other day and none of it is cohesive or has any structure to it.

Their branding changes all the time and nobody REALLY knows exactly what they are an expert at. Some days they are a motivational person and some days they are a business expert. All the indications are that they aren't sure themselves and this tends to turn people away.

If you are sending unclear messages out to the universe, this could be the very reason you are not getting the results you really want in your business. A person who toots their own horn, but doesn't have anyone else tooting it for them is also very easy to spot.

If you are new in business or you have been at it for a while without the desired results, make sure you are clear on a few things before you confuse your entire market:

- What EXACT gift do you have that changes people's lives?
- What testimonials do you have of others singing your praises?
- How are you different from everyone else doing what you do?
- Are you undercutting your prices just to get people to work with you?
- Are you constantly working on building up a loyal following?
- Do you have SEVERAL products and services for people to consume?

Always remember that a successful business person finds ways to profit in their business consistently.

If your sales are intermittent, the business will never sustain you full-time. And the only way to profit consistently is to have multiple offers all of the time!

Day 2: Today's Thought

An imperfect action is better than no action at all.
Vicki Irvin

Day 3: Reviewing Feedback

I posted a quote on Facebook that everyone seemed to enjoy this week. Someone told me she called a friend and got her voicemail.

Here is what the voicemail said, "Please leave a message. If you do not receive a return call it's because I am making some changes in my life and you're one of them."

I thought that was hilarious, but more importantly it is unfortunately something that we all have to do from time to time in order to keep moving forward and making sure we are surrounded by positive people!

Now I don't know what month of the year you're going to be reading this but it doesn't really matter!

I bet back at the start of the year you set up an action plan and had some things you vowed to do in your business this year.

Whether that was last week or several months ago, I wonder where you are in the process? I hope you have some great things to report!

However, I have been knee-deep reviewing feedback from clients about how they are getting on with their businesses and I am going to share some common themes that I can see are keeping many people stuck.

I am going to list them and you can check off where you are.

Underneath each roadblock, I will tell you what you HAVE to do in order to move forward. Without learning these things for yourself or hiring someone who can do it for you, your results will not be satisfactory!

1.   Nobody knows how to find you and your product/service.
You are not generating any traffic to your website or landing page. Work on a plan to get new leads from multiple sources. Gain an online presence with your website, and drive traffic to it.

2.   Your sales copy on your offers is not good.
Learn how to write copy and sales messages that are proven to sell using direct response marketing. Hiring a copywriter is very expensive; so if you can't do that, then learn how to write effectively to sell for yourself.

3.   You are relying on one method of traffic for your business.
You must diversify the ways in which you bring new leads/prospects to your business. Never rely on only one source – fatal mistake. Come up with multiple sources.

4.   You are marketing to the wrong people.
Do market research to determine who your exact consumer is; do not make your own assumptions. If you are marketing to the wrong audience you are dead in the water.

5.   You are not giving your clients what they want.
You are not in tune with what products and services your clients want. You are making assumptions on what YOU think is best for them and what YOU think they need. Find out what they WANT and not NEED by asking them for feedback. Design your business around their answers.

These remain some of the top roadblocks for business owners.

If you can get these five things right, you are well on your way. We have a saying that if you keep on doing what you are doing, you will keep on getting what you have got!

Day 4: Today's Action

Find a pair of pants that you can no longer fit into and resolve to make changes in your lifestyle so that you will fit into them.

Day 5: Winning the Entrepreneurial War

I got an email today from Dan Kennedy, whose teachings I follow very closely. He stated that we are in an entrepreneurial war! I couldn't agree more!

Anybody can make money in their business in a good economy without a whole lot of effort. But when the economy changes or things are thrown off one little bit, if you do not have a system or the skillset to shift your business model, then you will probably be going out of business.

A smart entrepreneur arms herself with the tools she needs to combat any conditions. And then she gets into HUSTLE-MODE!

As an entrepreneur you have to stay hungry! You have to stay in hustle-mode, even when the economy is good. You have to do MORE than your competitors are doing and you have to plug up all the holes in your business.

And another important thing… you MUST learn how to attract paying clients. Wealth attraction is a mindset. If you do not invest in yourself or your business, then you can't expect clients and customers to invest in you. That is the real law of attraction!

Take a moment to reflect on your business today. Have you been investing in yourself and your education? Do you have a qualified coach or mentor? Are you staying on top of your game and ahead of your competitors?

If you are doing these things, you should be prospering. But if you are NOT doing those things, chances are you are not making the money you should be. And nothing will change for you until you start living in a wealthy mindset and attracting wealth.

Day 8: Today's Thought

The secret of getting ahead is getting started.
Agatha Christie

Day 9: Turning Prospects Into Clients

I just came off a coaching call with a client and she was telling me she was having trouble turning her prospects into clients.

Let's face it. That's a common issue. I get women all the time saying people seem to be interested, but they just won't buy.

Well many times it is because you have spent absolutely ZERO time working on building a relationship with your prospects. I have said it before and I will say it again. Selling your products and services is a process very similar to dating a man. Let me show the parallels; pay close attention.

You are at the party with your girlfriends, looking and feeling great. You are all dressed up in a beautiful outfit; your hair and make-up are flawless.

Men have been approaching you all night, most of them giving you phony lines you have heard before and many of them offending you with their direct approach. Some even looking you up and down with only one thing on their mind! What a turn off!

But then, as soon as you were giving up hope of meeting a quality man, out of nowhere he approaches. He walks up confidently. He looks you in the eye, smiles and says, "Good evening. I wanted to tell you that you look beautiful tonight. How are you enjoying the party so far?"

Finally, a man who doesn't devour you with his eyes but instead he pays you a compliment and strikes up a friendly and normal conversation. What a relief! You relax, you return the smile and then you engage in friendly talk.

Before he leaves he asks if he may have your number to call you some time and get to know you better. You agree and happily give him those seven digits. All hope is not gone. There are still nice guys out there who know how to respectfully approach a woman. You find yourself eagerly anticipating his call. It has been a great night!

Sound familiar? Of course it does. Well the process is the same when you begin communicating with a prospect.

When someone is interested in your product or service, they may opt into your website, or start reading your blog or ezine. If you are on Facebook, they may join your group or fan page. At that time, it is YOUR job to begin to build a healthy relationship with them.

That does NOT mean go in for the kill and immediately try to sell them. That is overwhelming and pushy just like those jerky guys out there on the dating scene. Instead, speak their language and offer great information and content they can actually use. Something that makes them say, "Wow, she really knows her stuff."

Talk about yourself and let your prospects get to know you. Don't bother trying to be Miss Ultra Professional who is untouchable. Be a real person; infuse some personality into what you are writing.

People like to do business with people they like; who seem to be just like them. That is a proven fact.

Talk about your dog or cat; people can relate. The most important thing is to work on building trust and staying in communication.

When that prospect is ready to buy, they will remember YOU, the awesome business lady who gives so much value for free and who is so down to earth.

And if you ever forget, just think about that dating scene! Treat your prospects how you want Mr. Right to treat you when he first walks up! Works like a charm!

Day 10: Today's Action

Track how you spend every 15 minutes of your time today and see how many hours each day you are truly productive.

Day 11: Choosing Your Friends

Here's a little question for you today. Who are you hanging around with?

I know you have heard it all before. "You are a product of who you choose to hang around with." BUT, do you REALLY believe it?

I used to be of the belief that it didn't matter who you hung out with, you were still your own person and would do your own thing. BOY was I wrong!

Choosing to hang out with like-minded people who have goals, dreams and motivation can make all the difference in your world!

We all have them. Various groups and subsets of friends who we have connected with during different periods of our life. Childhood friends, college friends, friends from work or church, etc.

And I bet they are all different!

Some people, no matter how hard they try to dig themselves out of negativity, can't seem to shake it.

They wake up negative and are on a daily mission to see who they can pull down with them. Pretty sad, but oh so common!

Some people are born into constant drama and can't get away from it. In fact if there is no drama, they can't seem to function; it's almost as if chaos is a MUST have in their lives.

And although you may really love the friends OR family who are full of drama and negativity, after a while it will bring you down. It will suck the life out of you and leave you exhausted... if you allow them to.

See, I believe that nobody has the right to impose their negativity on you. If they choose to stay in that space, then fine. But to bring someone else down and expect them to indulge in the same destructive behavior is totally unfair.

But how about when you are in the presence of people who are truly happy for your successes in life, no matter how big or small?

How does it feel to get encouragement and genuine well wishes from people who truly care?

You can't help but to stay motivated and feel like you have someone you can lean on, right? It propels you to do even more!

It is not your job to entertain miserable people. It is your job to reach your goals by staying positive, supported and having people who want to see you do your thing!

If you find yourself struggling to find people who make you feel good, it is time to clean house. You deserve the BEST environment possible!

Day 12: Today's Thought
You are never too old to set another goal or to dream a new dream.
C.S. Lewis

Day 15: Your Sales Prevention Department

This past weekend I went to the UK for the UFC fight and a special Mastermind session with Ken McCarthy and some brilliant internet marketers! The information was fabulous and being put to use right away!

My coaching clients are going to love me for the new money-boosting tips they can add to their business in a matter of hours! Internet marketing is such a male dominated field, but that is all going to change, trust me.

Ok, so what is up with the Sales Prevention department so many people have built into their businesses without even realizing it?

Everywhere I go, I pay special attention to the customer service I receive and make a note of how many businesses are turning away customers who are ready to pay! I tried to order something today on the phone and the lady said she would get back to me in a day! I had my credit card out and everything!

A month ago my husband and I went to Best Buy to order some new cameras and he asked if there was any new technology or equipment he could add to enhance his purchase and the salesclerk told him – and I quote – "Not that I know of." It happens all the time.

First, if you have employees handling your service, you had better ensure they are trained and know that they are being monitored. Employees receive pay checks. They are not all that interested in repeat customers or selling your clients on more services.

Why? Because they do not see what is in it for them. Whether they sell one or 15 of your products is not going to change their pay check unless they receive a commission. See the lack of motivation?

If you were to monitor the amount of money your employees have turned away for your business, you would be sick to your stomach.

In the UK this weekend, I met a wonderful man and musician Chuck who told us a story of how a woman was selling water filtration systems.

She was giving a presentation to his friend who half way through it, told him he didn't need to see anymore and was ready to buy. But she insisted that he needed to go through with the entire presentation.

Further, she said she wanted to prove how great her product was by searching online and showing him what others were saying about the product. Well guess what? Her searched turned up a bunch of negative feedback on the system.

He quickly put his credit card away and needless to say she did NOT make that sale. How is THAT for sales prevention! When he was ready to buy, she should have let him. When someone is ready to buy from you, LET THEM, right then and there.

It only takes a few minutes for a customer to cool off and decide to spend their money on something else.

So what is going on in YOUR business that could be preventing ready and willing customers from paying you?

- Poor employees?
- Lack of systems?
- Do you promptly get back to people when they reach out to you?

Think long and hard about it. You may have a Sales Prevention Office built right into your business and you didn't even know it!

Day 16: Today's Action
Reward yourself with a relaxing massage.

Day 17: Getting Your Message Right

I've just been flicking through one of my favorite magazines and, of course, I try to pay a bit of attention to the ads as well as the content.

Do you ever wonder why so many people are selling the same products and services yet only a handful of people in any one industry really stand out with brand and name recognition?

It is because they have spent time working on positioning themselves in the market place and you have got to do the same thing.

Don't get frustrated because you feel like you have been plugging away and not making progress. Most likely you are plugging away at all the wrong things. It is about working RIGHT not hard. Now, you may be sick and tired of hearing me say this, but it all boils down to your marketing prowess; my story will never change.

The "economic slowdown" excuse is invalid because people are still spending money on what they see value in. If your marketing message is strong enough to make people see the value in your product or service then you too will be making money. The economy definitely makes people tighten their purse strings and focus on what they can and can't do without. But believe me, if you are a good marketer, you will be on the "can't do without" list.

Let's get back to the basics here. You must have the RIGHT MESSAGE, THE RIGHT MARKET and use the RIGHT MEDIA.

If anything goes wrong in this sequence you are limiting your potential greatly. What good is a great message to the right market if you aren't reaching that market with the right media? What good is using great media to reach the right market if your message sucks?

So go back and figure these things out. If your marketing message does not move people to some kind of action, you have to fix it. There has ALWAYS got to be a call to action.

If your message does not solve a problem for people then you have to fix that because you are supposed to be their solution. If your message is not overcoming the common objections of buyers in your industry, you have got to fix that, and yes it is your responsibility to know what they are.

If you are using media to advertise that does not reach your ideal demographic, your message is falling on deaf ears who could not care less.

Day 18: Today's Thought

If you want to conquer fear, don't sit home and think about it. Go out and get busy.
Dale Carnegie

Day 19: Your Most Important Investment

Sometimes even a Superwoman can get a little frustrated!

For me, it often comes about when I'm doing my best to encourage a client to push themselves to the next level.

The thing is I can give them all the technical knowledge they would ever need to go out and make their business thrive. But it won't happen unless they are willing to invest in themselves and go to the next level.

The people you see who are successful are working non-stop and staying educated. To attain a certain level of success, you MUST do extraordinary things. Extraordinary results only come when you work RIGHT.

Notice I did not say work hard. Working right beats working hard any day. If you can attach yourself to a successful person who has a proven success model you can follow, that is half the battle conquered right there.

There is no need to go out and reinvent the wheel when someone proves to you their model yields results.

If you are okay with being ordinary, then by all means, that is fine. But if you are looking to be extraordinary then there is no way you will do it until you realize you have to invest in learning what is making the successful people so darn successful.

I personally spend thousands upon thousands of dollars to learn from the top marketers in the country each year. My mentors are well known for their success and for making others successful. My husband and successful friends do the same thing.

Ask any successful person you know about their own investment in their ongoing education and they will tell you the same thing. There just ain't no short cuts!

So before you go spinning your wheels and getting frustrated because you are not where you want to be in your business, ask yourself what you have done to get there.

You can't be cheap with your own education. Stop investing in shoes, cars, designer clothes, and fancy vacations that aren't doing a thing for your bank account and financial status.

Start investing in learning how to generate the kind of income that will change not only your life, but the life of your family.

Day 22: Today's Action

Contact an expert in your market to interview them for your blog.

Day 23: Meeting Real Needs

I've been putting the finishing touches on a new product I'm going to be launching soon.

Before I even started working on it, I spent time talking to my customers and finding out their problems and worries.

Now here's the thing. These days everybody wants to make money with their business online and jump into the world of internet marketing. It is attractive to so many people because it gives you the impression of just sending an email or two and having money just drop into your bank account.

While that is kinda how it works, there are specific steps to make sure it does. There is a right and a wrong way to market your business and there is also a system to it. If you have not studied and mastered a proven system of internet marketing then chances are you are not making that much money as an internet marketer with your products.

That does not mean that you can't. It just means you have to understand the psychology behind what converts a prospect to a customer.

If you chose to skip this step and not gain a clear understanding of why the system works, then you won't be in business long. Trying to short cut the process is one of the top reasons so many women entrepreneurs fail in business.

Regardless if you are a coach, consultant, or network marketer, your products and services can outsell your competition any day if you take the time to learn how to market. First let's look at some ways you can make money online. Write down which categories your business, product or service fits into:

- **Selling things**: This includes any type of tangible product
- **Selling information:** eBooks, videos, audio, membership sites, or information sites
- **Combination**: Combining any number of tangible items that are making money

- **Product**: Products you have created and have permission to sell to others
- **Information**: Information on your field of expertise/industry you have created and have permission to sell or license
- **Affiliate**: This simply means that you are promoting, marketing, and/or selling someone else's product or information for a fee or portion of the sale amount
- **Ads:** Perhaps a membership site where you drive targeted traffic and you have others paying you to advertise on your site

Can you see your business fitting into any of these categories? If so, you can create your information products and make money; that is the good news!

Confused about what to do next? Does it all seem too overwhelming for you? It doesn't have to be! After creating your information product, you need someone to market to, correct? Where do these prospects come from?

Well, they had better be coming from your efforts at building up your list. In this business your list is your golden egg. Your list should be guarded and protected with your life, nurtured like you nurture and tend to a baby, and the relationship should be cultivated and given lots of attention.

I am still amazed at how many women entrepreneurs have awesome products and services but don't know how to attract clients or how to sell them properly. Another step that cannot be avoided or your business will be doomed.

So building a list of qualified prospects is a must.

Day 24: Today's Thought

Our greatest weakness lies in giving up. The most certain way to succeed is always to try just one more time.
Thomas A. Edison

Day 25: Being All You Can Be

I'm just preparing for a trip to Vegas. Many women ask me why I travel so much and just what I am up to when I travel. Well I believe my frequent travel actually has a lot to do with my success!

I believe another vital factor is "getting your mind right." Now some people think this is a bunch of mumbo jumbo nonsense, huh?

Well I used to think the same thing when I was starting out as an entrepreneur. I wanted to skip all the talks about belief systems and surrounding myself with the "right" people... blah, blah, blah!

I quickly learned that I could have all the technical knowledge I needed, BUT if I didn't have my mind right, surround myself with positive people who pushed me and I didn't believe in my full potential, I would get absolutely NOWHERE.

See, being an entrepreneur means you are entering a lonely world where few talk your language. How many times have you tried talking about your business to family or friends who just looked at you like you had two heads? Or how many times did people tell you that you were nuts and that you need to stick to your day job? THAT is the reality of the world of entrepreneurship.

Tip number one...YOU MUST BECOME IMMUNE TO CRITICISM to survive! If you take every negative comment or rejection personally, you will crumble. Tough skin is in order and not allowing anyone to take you off of your path is a must.

Tip number two, I'll keep for a couple of days!

Day 26: Today's Action

Arrange lunch with your best friend and then take the rest of the afternoon off so that you can relax and make the most of it.

Day 29: Continuing to Learn

So here's where I left off a couple of days ago – tip number two.

Thinking you can learn and do it all on your own is a myth. I don't care how focused you are, when you do not invest in your own education, you will never get off the ground or you will stall and never realize your full potential or level of success.

Every single successful person you know and admire has coaches and mentors to guide them to the next level. They all invest in themselves to continue to learn and grow their business; there are no exceptions to the rule.

When you see me traveling, I am typically on a business trip investing in my education with one of my mentors and I have several. And yes my investments pay off 100 times over with the skills and knowledge I am able to learn and apply that in turn increase my business profits.

And I have become a master at finding ways to turn business trips into fun as well; nothing wrong with killing two birds with one stone! I have had to show clients how they CAN afford to invest in themselves.

Money is tight for everyone, but there is always a way to invest in yourself. It is amazing how many women entrepreneurs will skimp on education to increase their bank accounts for elaborate vacations, designer clothes and shoes, and useless spending on non-income generating items.

You can't have it both ways. Either you are serious about your business, or you wish to just bask in the meaningless fly by night pleasures of life that do nothing more than drain your bank account and put you further in debt.

The serious woman entrepreneur knows the difference and makes the sacrifice. Once you are making the money, THEN you can justify treating and rewarding yourself.

So if you are TRULY serious about your business, you have got to dedicate yourself to following a serious model and blueprint for success. Skipping steps does not work and it is another reason so few women entrepreneurs are realizing their full potential.

Day 30: Today's Thought

What you get by achieving your goals is not as important as what you become by achieving your goals.
Henry David Thoreau

Looking Back and Looking Forward

What are the top five things you have learned this month?

1.

2.

3.

4.

5.

What are the top five actions you will take next month?

1.

2.

3.

4.

5.

MONTH 5

Day 1: Knowing Your Target Market

Today I've been busy working on critiques that I offered as a bonus to the first ten ladies who submitted their information to me.

The purpose of the critique was to show how often women entrepreneurs are off the mark on who their target market is. Just about 100% of the submissions were off the mark.

Most women entrepreneurs have not been taught the secrets to market research or they are unaware how important and crucial this step is. But that is okay and something we are going to change.

I also promised to pick one submission and use it as a case study so that everyone could benefit.

Here is the one I chose to share so you can see how the trained eye can see other opportunities that most would not be aware existed.

I asked for three things:

- Website
- Who you think your ideal client/customer is
- An explanation of your product or service

Her explanation as to what she does:

"I am a Life & Career Empowerment Coach. My ultimate goal is to help each client change their life to change their legacy by empowering them to create more fulfillment in their personal and professional lives through creating a Success Model that will help each client take control over their lives and purposefully navigate their way to success, no matter the arena in life. My ideal client is small business owners."

I commented that her explanation, had I asked her at a networking event, would have left me confused and unclear and you only have a few seconds to capture a potential client's interest. I suggested something more like this:

"I am a life and empowerment coach who customizes a plan of success and action for my clients based on their lifestyle and personal / professional aspirations and goals."

After looking at her website and getting a feel for what she does, I felt she could help a lot more people than just small business owners which she indicated was her target market.

I felt she could open up a whole new stream of income by reaching out to others and here is what I told her:

"Too narrow! I am sure there are employees who are burnt out from their 9-5 jobs and are looking for a career change or to go into business for themselves. With your help, you could assist them in developing a transition plan to reach these goals as well as help them figure out what their true desires are.

That opens up a whole new target market for you. EVERYBODY has a passion inside of them they want to release and many need direction from someone like you to actually do it! Not just small business owners."

This woman entrepreneur seems very powerful and passionate to me and I know so many others could benefit from what she has to offer.

By going after more than just small business owners, she opens up her business to a major increase in revenue stream.

Keep in mind these are just quick examples and they can and should be properly researched and honed.

Day 2: Today's Thought

Knowing is not enough; we must apply.
Willing is not enough; we must do.
Johann Wolfgang von Goethe

Day 3: The Skill of Copywriting

I've spent this morning working on the latest issue of my weekly ezine E-volve. I love writing it and I enjoy the feedback I get through it. But I also find it easy to write as I took the trouble to learn the skill of copywriting.

If you choose to make email marketing your primary source of communicating with your prospects and clients, then you have got to learn how to write copy.

Copywriting is a skill that every serious marketer has got to dive into. See, it's one thing to have a message that you want to get out, but if nobody bothers to open up your email, your message will never get read.

So why do some emails get opened with anticipation and others just get deleted or skipped over? Because of the email subject line and how it is written.

Writing compelling, cliff hanger subject lines gets your emails opened at a much higher rate than drab humdrum ones.

What would you be more likely to open?

- "Valentine's Day Special Offer For Him"

or

- "Love, You, Him… Tonight?"

I think we can all agree the second subject line is the more compelling of the two. In a world where people are constantly inundated with emails and spam, what are you going to do to stand out from the rest?

Thought has to go into this every time you send communication to your list or your sales will not be where they should be. The same goes for writing copy that is intended to introduce your product or service for sale. Just explaining in detail what your product or service does is not enough to get anyone to buy from you.

It is your job to explain the benefits and features of your business and how you can solve a problem for them. There is a clear and concise formula for writing copy the right way, and it is the difference between people who are able to make sales versus those who are not.

If we were to take two different companies selling the same product equally as great, who would convert the most sales? The one who writes the best copy will be the winner every time.

As you know by now, I frequently invest in myself and my education and copywriting was one of those investments that have paid off for me 100 times over!

Day 4: Today's Action

Book a hotel room for the day and then catch up on all your incomplete tasks.

Day 5: The Superwoman Lifestyle

Wow this has been a super busy week but I can remember when I'd be exhausted doing half as much.

That was before I discovered the Superwoman Lifestyle. This is all about having balance in your life, or at least something that resembles it!

For us women in business, striving to fulfill our dreams and missions, while taking care of our children and families and OURSELVES, has been a huge struggle for a long time.

Perhaps you don't get the support you need in these areas; I know how that can be. It's hard to push forward every day when you feel like you are alone and nobody understands.

That is why your success in each aspect of your life greatly depends on who you surround yourself with and the environment you draw your strength from.

Many, many women don't have a community or environment of like-minded people who "get it."

Do you? Do you have someone who says, "I understand your business, I understand your drive of being an entrepreneur"… or how about, "I understand you want to get healthier and find more time for yourself and your family." It's hard to accomplish these goals when you often stand alone.

No matter how great someone's life looks from the outside, no matter how successful you think they are, as women we all have stories of struggle.

But I do know that together, side by side, we can push each other to rise above to even greater heights.

Day 8: Today's Thought

Every worthwhile accomplishment, big or little, has its stages of drudgery and triumph; a beginning, a struggle and a victory.
Ghandi

Day 9: Why Testimonials Matter

One of my clients has just sent me a wonderful testimonial talking about the way her life has turned around since we started working together.

I was so pleased because I didn't even ask her to send it.

The thing is nobody cares all that much about what you have to say about yourself; it is all about what others have to say about you! Once you grasp this concept, you will quickly realize how important it is to constantly capture great testimonials from your clients... with video!

Serious entrepreneurs will whip out a flip camera ANYWHERE and start filming things to promote their business. If you are shopping in Walmart and someone walks up to you and says, "Hey, I used your product and boy was it awesome," what would YOU do?

Wanna know what I would do? Well, I would say, "Great Susie, mind saying that one more time for me on my flip camera?"

When your products or services provide great value to others, they become raving fans, and raving fans help promote your business. Gathering great testimonials should be a consistent and important component of your business.

I remember going to my friend John Hall's spa in Virginia. John has studied marketing for his business under my husband and me for years. Well when I tried to leave his spa he literally blocked my path with his flip camera and told me it was time for a testimonial!

Imagine the horror of having just gotten a facial and having on no make-up with a video right in your face! (Not cute)

But what could I do? As a business owner, he was doing his job and even bigger than that, I taught him to always do it!

See you can spend all day talking about how great your product or service is, but potential clients or customers don't want to hear it from only you; they want to know what other people who have tried your stuff feel about it. Does it really work? Does it work well? What were the benefits? That is called social proof. Without it, you are at a disadvantage because people just will not be convinced if you yourself are your only raving fan.

See, even a BAD video is better than no video at all. You don't need to be a trained videographer; flip cameras are so easy, even my young son knows how to operate it!

It is a PROVEN FACT that using great video and video testimonials in your marketing will increase your sales conversions by leaps and bounds.

If you are not using video to market your business, you are behind the times and you are leaving money on the table! So if you do not have a flip camera, it is the best investment you can make! If you do have one, but have been lax in using it, then dust it off and get busy!

Day 10: Today's Action

Write down everything you eat for the next three days and consider whether you should change your diet.

Day 11: The Power of Networking

Today I was at a great networking event where I met some super interesting people.

However, I can't help noticing that some people get it completely wrong at these events. What about you? Are you turning people off?

Please say you aren't one of those people who shove your business card in someone's face and actually think they are going to call you. I find that people just do not know how to network and connect with people the RIGHT way.

Networking does not mean walking up to someone with an elevator speech on your business and what it can do for them. In fact most people have it backwards. Instead of doing all the talking, try listening.

Listening isn't easy for any of us; it is a skill that you must practice and learn. Think about the arguments you get into with your spouse or friend. While they are presenting their side of things, you are not listening or taking in what they are saying, instead you are busy preparing your defense in your head, ready to pounce back as soon as they take a breath!

How do I know? Because I was guilty of it too, until someone showed me how to be a good listener!

Let me share a story with you that will bring this into focus. One of my mentors James Malinchak is a master at connecting with people. He told me that when you wish to network/connect with someone you have to offer them something first. Your focus should be on how you can serve them with no strings attached.

James recently connected with Dr. Bill Dorfman; he is the celebrity dentist from Extreme Makeover and also the creator of Zoom teeth whitening. Well as you can imagine, Dr. Dorfman is worth millions. But his focus is on raising money for his charity, the Leap Foundation, which focuses on helping children; that is his passion.

So when he met James, James offered to help him raise money for his charity.

James raised over $100,000 at his live event in December and I was there to witness it all. Dr. Dorfman came to personally thank everyone who donated.

Well as you can imagine, Dr. Dorfman was SUPER impressed with what James was able to do in an hour of fundraising. In turn they have developed a great relationship and friendship. James was just on the TV show THE DOCTORS on CBS earlier this week with Dr. Dorfman. My point is that James served Dr. Dorfman first, a man worth over $170 million dollars and in turn Dr. Dorfman and James are now hanging tight! LOL.

None of this would have happened if James had run up to Dr. Dorfman asking him to do something for HIM. It doesn't pay to be self-serving all the time.

Day 12: Today's Thought

Twenty years from now you will be more disappointed by the things that you didn't do than by the ones you did do. So throw off the bowlines. Catch the trade winds in your sails. Explore. Dream. Discover.
Mark Twain

Day 15: Value Yourself

I've just finished hosting a teleseminar and there was some great discussion and loads of really stimulating questions.

However, one of the things I can't help noticing is that we women short-change ourselves when it comes to talking about what we do for people.

Are you passionate about your product or service? Do you KNOW that people can benefit from what you have to offer? I'm sure the answer is yes. And if the answer is yes, then why are you short-changing yourself?

So many women entrepreneurs are afraid to even charge for their services. And if they do charge, they are devaluing their services by charging nominal fees out of fear or thinking their prices are too high and nobody would ever buy.

If this is you, then I can tell you right now that your business is probably not profitable or anywhere near where it should be considering the worth of your product. You are in business to make money, not to run a hobby... at least I hope!

Having a successful and profitable business starts with you believing in what you do and being able to look people square in the eye with confidence when you quote your prices.

The worst position to be in when you have competitors is the "cheapest" in town. The best position is to be the highest priced, a concept many have a hard time wrapping their mind around.

Many businesses have gone right OUT of business by trying to undercut their competitors' prices – thinking customers will flock to them because they are cheaper.

While that may work for a minute, the success is short-lived and they quickly realize they cannot sustain running a business at cheap prices. I have seen it happen time and time again.

If people cannot afford you at the price point that you have set based on what you are delivering, the quality of your product or service and what makes you profitable, then they are NOT your target client or customer. Don't adjust your price; adjust the target market you are marketing to.

And for those of you who have been giving your stuff away for nothing and "helping" people, it is time to stop.

While we all like to give back and help out, rarely do people value anything you just give them because they have not invested their good hard-earned resources and it is easy to blow off.

But when people have "skin in the game" and make an investment, they are more apt to actually work so they can see a return on their investment. So giving it all away is really not helping anyone at all, now is it?

Value yourself. Value your skills, value what you have that can change someone's life. If YOU don't value your business, you can't expect anyone else to.

Day 16: Today's Action

Identify something about your business that would be interesting to others and issue a press release about it.

Day 17: Letting Subscribers Go

I just received a notification from someone who opted out of my list and she provided the reason why. You see I recently sent out an email with a headline that read "You Are So Cheap."

Here is what she said: *"Your emails are not cute. You are breeding negativity and negativity spreads disease."*

She sounds pretty ticked off right? Well the fact of the matter is that I use compelling headlines to get my subscribers to read the darn great information I write for them each week!

Every time I write, I think about what subject line I can use to get people to even open up my email. And if my headlines weren't ticking some people off, then I am NOT doing my job!

See the fact of the matter is, the woman who wrote that I was being negative, never bothered to read my email.

If she had read it, she would see that my ezine was all about pricing your products accordingly and knowing your worth. But she was someone who signed up on my list for probably not the right reasons at all, and in turn is not my target client.

The fact is if your marketing is not ticking some people off, then you aren't doing your job! Sounds crazy right? Well, here is the truth of the matter.

As an entrepreneur it is your job to deliver content the people on your list have signed up for. Your market will appreciate your information (if it is good) and will even be able to use some of the things you show them. How often you choose to communicate with your list is up to you, but it should be often enough that you are able to build a rapport with them.

Anyone who chooses to "opt out" of your list is not interested in what you are doing for whatever reason. And that is okay.

I remember when I was first starting out, I would get so upset if someone opted out of my list, I really took it personally... until my coaches and mentors told me that was normal and they aren't my target client anyway.

What is the point in having someone on your list who isn't interested in what you do? NONE!

No matter how great your ezine, newsletter or blog is, nobody will ever get to see it if YOU do not write compelling subject lines and headlines that spark their curiosity enough to even open the darn thing!

Day 18: Today's Thought

The best and most beautiful things in the world cannot be seen or even touched – they must be felt with the heart.
Helen Keller

Day 19: Taking Giant Leaps

I am always super-excited to hear about my client success stories so it was great to hear of one of my clients being featured in a spread in a national magazine.

The fact is every woman has something special about her business and with the right specialized knowledge, the sky is the limit on what you can do and what you can earn!

Are you taking big leaps in your business or small baby steps? Baby steps are great IF that is genuinely all you can do. But the fact of the matter is that you are capable of taking big leaps.

I know that you are passionate about succeeding in your business. I know that you often can't sleep at night because you are thinking about ways to enhance your business.

How do I know? Because I do the same thing all the time, and many of my sleepless nights are spent thinking about how I can help YOU leap to success.

When I was featured in the movie "The Phenomenon" it was all about entrepreneurs who accomplished more in the last 12 months than they had in the last 12 years. Long gone is the philosophy that you have to slave away hours and hours and work as hard as possible to enjoy the fruits of your labor.

That was the old way of thinking from generations and generations ago. Today with the proven success systems and technology, you can leap to mega-success in record time... IF you do things the right way and take the time to study a blueprint that works.

What may seem commonplace to you for your business is often mind-blowing to other people.

So you may need someone to look at your business with "fresh" eyes and show you additional ways to profit and other approaches to take.

Day 22: Today's Action

Carry out a random act of kindness – do something nice for anyone without expecting anything in return.

Day 23: The Business You Are Really In

I've just come off a coaching call with a client. She's great at what she does but the struggle she's been facing is one of the most common I see.

You see, success in business is not just about being good at what you do.

I know you have heard me say it before, but I'm going to say it again. As a business owner you are in the business of sales and marketing.

Marketing, I know many of you are comfortable with, but sales is scary to a lot of people. Nobody wants to seem too pushy and the thought of having to "sell" to someone leaves many women shaking in their stilettos!

But it doesn't have to be that way. Did you know that there is an art and science to selling ethically by motivating and persuading your clients to buy from you? Yup, there sure is!

Let's face it. Whatever product or service you are trying to get prospects and customers to buy from you, many times it takes a lot of convincing.

Now I am not talking about trying to sell sand in the desert to someone when you know they don't need it. I am talking about KNOWING for a fact that someone can benefit from your services in a positive way.

I will use myself as an example... I know for a fact my coaching program for women entrepreneurs can change their lives and their bank accounts. I have knowledge and skills that, if and when applied, are proven to make people money. So if I am speaking with a potential client who is on the fence about whether or not to work with me, guess what my job is? TO CONVINCE HER! And just how do I do that without coming across as too "sales-y?"

Well there is a whole bunch of things that I need to do – starting with showing her the benefits of working with me. I also show her other real life people I have helped make money for and how THEY have benefitted from working with me. Always remember that what someone ELSE has to say about you is far more powerful than anything you can ever say about yourself!

That is why having testimonials and case studies is so important; they help make your case for you. Another thing you need to do is over-deliver!

Go above and beyond with your offers and provide great value that makes you stand out from your competition. It won't go unnoticed because people definitely do compare your offers to others.

And here is a biggie... you must learn how to overcome the most common objections in your industry that prevent people from buying and address them head on before they can even bring them up. That is why doing market research and knowing the thought patterns of your market are so vital to your business success.

The woman entrepreneur who masters this system of ethical persuasion is the woman who will thrive in business.

Day 24: Today's Thought
Don't judge each day by the harvest you reap but
by the seeds that you plant.
Robert Louis Stevenson

Day 25: Traffic + Conversion = Cash

Chatting with a prospective new client today, I heard the line that really sets me off sometimes!

That line is, "But Vicki, my business if different."

I have to say that it does not matter what business you are in; there is a formula that works for ANY business I have come across. It's a basic formula that you have to master to prosper in business. I suggest you write this down someplace where you can see it every day:

Traffic + Conversion= Cash

Looks and sounds simple right? Well the sad truth is few women entrepreneurs know how to make this formula work for their business.

The system I am always talking about is centered on this concept and this concept only.

Once I learned how to drive traffic to my website, blogs, social media sites, etc., I then learned a system of converting that traffic from what are called "prospects" to actual customers or clients.

Once they become customers, that equals cash.

There are proven strategies on how to perform each step of the formula that, whenever applied correctly, will translate into money for your business.

Any successful marketer knows this system, but unfortunately that means mostly men! That's why I have taken the time to break it all down in our language. It took me FIVE years of hanging out with the top marketers in the country (and sometimes out of the country) to learn this stuff – and being practically the only woman was brutal!

But it sure paid off for me, and soon it will for you, too!

I'll be talking more about those steps and strategies on other days. Today I simply want you to focus on that proven formula for success.

Day 26: Today's Action

Add pop-ups to your website to collect more email addresses.

Day 29: What Do You Really Do?

I'm overwhelmed by all the fabulous testimonials for this week's Superwoman coaching call. We had a great discussion on the topic of "Are you SURE you know what it is that you do?"

I've mentioned before that many women entrepreneurs have a hard time explaining what their product or service is all about in a clear, concise, confident and succinct way. Sounds basic and simple, but few people have this down to a science.

You must carve out and design your marketing message so that when someone walks up to you and says, "What is it that you do?" you are able to rattle it off easily and quickly leaving the person knowing exactly what you have to offer rather than confused.

Now we have work to do if you are unsure of what to say, but that is okay. That is an indication that you aren't quite clear yourself in what direction you want to go with your business. Perhaps you have more than one idea or concept that you are trying to merge together that doesn't quite fit into the same business model.

Maybe you are holding onto something that you need to let go of. I know how it can be when you think you have a great idea, but it just doesn't work out. You need someone to help you let it go so you can move on and progress. The reason having a clear message is so important is because you have to know who your target market is.

You can't hone in on your target market if you aren't clear on your own services. And trust me when I say people will know the difference between someone who has it together and someone who does not, just based on how you communicate what you do.

Here are some questions to ask yourself about your business that you must be able to answer:

1. I am in the business of_____.
2. My target market is comprised of the following demographic_____.
3. The results you will attain as a result of my product/service are_____.
4. My business is unique from my competitors because_____.
5. My product/service is valuable because_____.

There are of course many more questions about your business you should be able to easily answer, but these are a great start. Go ahead and see what you come up with.

If you struggle or hesitate to answer any of them, then you have to do some work on getting clear on your direction. You won't be able to sell yourself to other people until you are confident and clear on what you do and that means selling yourself first!

Day 30: Today's Thought

I believe in pink. I believe that laughing is the best calorie burner. I believe in kissing, kissing a lot. I believe in being strong when everything seems to be going wrong. I believe that happy girls are the prettiest girls. I believe that tomorrow is another day and I believe in miracles.
Audrey Hepburn

Looking Back and Looking Forward

What are the top five things you have learned this month?

1.

2.

3.

4.

5.

What are the top five actions you will take next month?

1.

2.

3.

4.

5.

MONTH 6

Day 1: Media and Marketing

I've mentioned before that I'm a big follower of Dan Kennedy. He is not only one of the world's greatest marketing gurus, but he has the ability to get straight to the point with a message.

I was just reading something very important from him on the subject of marketing.

He was pointing out that all these things like social media marketing, internet marketing, and info-marketing are not MARKETING. They are simply media. They are ways to deliver your marketing message.

While I already knew that, it dawned on me that many people do not and they are missing this basic concept.

What good is Facebook or Twitter if you do not have a good marketing message to promote? People are being lulled into a false sense of security with these media.

Yes, it is great that there are free ways to get your message out there but once again, if you lack the marketing know-how, they are useless.

The ONLY people making money using any type of media are those who have taken the time to learn a marketing system that works. How many different ways are you marketing your business? Facebook alone is not going to cut it.

You along with thousands of other people are all competing for the same client in a very public forum. Talk about competition!

- Do you know how to go to places that your competitors are not?
- Do you know how to protect your following from your competitors?
- Do you know how to talk to your prospects in a place that nobody else is hanging out?

Just adding one more media or marketing funnel to your campaign can make all the difference in the world. If I relied on just one way of marketing my business, I would be eating beans out of a can right now, and any other successful entrepreneur will tell you the same thing!

Day 2: Today's Thought

Change your thoughts and you change your world.
Norman Vincent Peale

Day 3: Joan Rivers Inspiration

I just saw a magazine article on Joan Rivers and was reminded that I heard her speak at a marketing conference some time ago.

Though she's a big personality, she was there because she is a smart businesswoman and has created an empire.

Reading the article brought back some of her words of wisdom that I noted at the time:

- Say "Yes" to every opportunity that comes your way
- Rise to the occasion no matter how scared or unsure you are
- Do not give up even when others count you out

She also said you have to be persistent; you can't be a successful entrepreneur without persistence. Finally, she said, if you don't have the will, drive or motivation, then go work for someone else!

Day 4: Today's Action

Find a top blog in your market and offer to write a guest post.

Day 5: Finding Time for You

Yesterday, Superwoman Lifestyle members were talking about how they are trying to make healthy eating a part of their daily routine like I have been advising.

Some have mastered it and others are still struggling to do it. The struggle comes from your time being limited. And, when you are pressed for time, it is easy to justify cutting corners on YOURSELF. But you are worth more than that.

With all that you do, you cannot sacrifice your health. Always remember that, the better care you take of yourself, the better care you can take of your loved ones. You deserve an hour a day a few times per week to do something beneficial for yourself. Every woman out there has an hour to focus on them. Find it and do it; no more excuses.

Day 8: Today's Thought

The possibilities and opportunities are endless for you and your business when you make the important and life-changing decision to learn the core principles and strategies of effective marketing.
Vicki Irvin

Day 9: Getting the Right Qualification

I've been doing some research for an upcoming event that I'm hosting and one thing I've noticed is how many really successful people never went to college.

I personally don't care whether you have a GED, PhD, BA, or BS. The only degree that matters is your MBA!

No I do NOT mean a Master's in Business Administration. MBA stands for MASSIVE BANK ACCOUNT. I first heard this from one of my coaches, James Malinchak, and boy was he on the money!

In the entrepreneurial world, degrees and where you went to school don't matter all that much. I have a Master's Degree, but I don't even bother to talk about it because nothing I learned in college taught me how to build, operate and market a successful business that can flourish in any economy.

I do think college is important, but it definitely is not what makes an entrepreneur successful.

In my research, I found that the most successful entrepreneurs focused on mastering a proven marketing system which, in turn, gave them their own Massive Bank Account.

Which MBA would YOU rather have?

Day 10: Today's Action

Make a commitment to do a teleseminar. Choose a topic, set the date and tell people about it.

Day 11: Making the Right Impression

I have three live events coming up and I am working like a maniac. It is going to be this way for the next few months so I guess I'd better get used to it.

One of my big lessons this week was noticing how important it is for any business owner to make the right connections with other people.

How you present and conduct yourself makes all the difference in the world when a person decides to use your services. Are you connecting with people or rubbing them the wrong way?

As an example, my awesome assistant told me someone called my office about the complimentary event I am putting together for women entrepreneurs this Saturday. The person was rude and demanding and clearly missed the fact that I am spending money to put on a complimentary event for women in the community.

While just about every other woman has thanked me for doing something that most would not, this person chose to put demands on ME! Imagine that?

I have learned from my mentors and own experiences a long time ago, that as soon as someone shows you who they really are through negativity, then you quickly make the decision that the person is not someone you want to work with or to bring around other positive people.

As an entrepreneur you have the option of deciding who you do and do not want to work with. Some clients are just not worth it and it defeats the purpose of you doing your own thing and having control over your own destiny. Never settle for working with someone who will make you miserable!

On the flip side, I also received a beautiful thank you note in the mail from an awesome business women who saw me present at an earlier event in Dallas.

This already very successful woman told me she learned so much from my presentation and thanked me for sharing. That brought a smile to my face.

It only takes a second to thank someone for sharing their time, expertise or kind words... and it goes a long way in making a connection that could one day turn out to be huge.

So as you go about your day or your business, make the decision to treat everyone with respect and remember that it only takes one person to put you on a path that can forever change your life.

Day 12: Today's Thought

I've been absolutely terrified every moment of my life
– and I've never let it keep me from doing a single thing I wanted to do.
Georgia O'Keeffe

Day 15: Three Things You Need

I hosted a great event this past weekend where I met some wonderful people and taught some powerful new strategies.

What always surprises me is that some people go to these events and nothing changes in their lives afterwards. It's almost like they think there is somewhere special that some of us are being given special information.

Here's the truth. There is no magic room!

So many people make excuses for themselves and why they are not prospering in their business the way they deserve. Nobody has an edge over you. Nobody has ANYTHING over you except possibly three things:

- The sheer will and motivation to succeed.
- The understanding that you must invest in yourself and learn real systems.
- The ability to take action and implement what you learn.

That is it, plain and simple. Once a person reaches the point where they understand this basic concept, they are well on their way.

Day 16: Today's Action

Redesign your workspace to make it more attractive and boost your energy levels.

Day 17: Making Progress

Man! I pulled my neck today lifting weights in the gym, but I think it is minor. I went a little nuts today because I missed a couple days of working out; whenever I do not work out, I panic a bit and then try to make up for it all the next time.

It takes 21 days to make or break a habit and working out is definitely a habit with me. As I've confessed before, I sometimes have a hard time seeing results in the mirror.

Everyone else can see results, but for some reason I can't. I lift weights and people talk about the muscles in my arms all the time, but I can't see it.

I talked to a couple of girlfriends and they said the same thing, they can't see their results, even though I can. I think that is a common issue with women.

We work hard, but our image never matches reality! Don't be discouraged by this. Find a pair of pants you can't fit anymore and use them as your benchmark or goal. Make it your goal to fit into that one particular pair of pants again.

This provides the proof of your hard work. Another good indicator of progress is pictures. Take before and after pictures, they will definitely be revealing!

Day 18: Today's Thought

The greatest mistake you can make in life is continually fearing you will make one.
Elbert Hubbard

Day 19: What's Wrong with Facebook?

Well I'm Miami-bound this weekend for some much needed rest with my family and friends! I have been working non-stop on so many projects and events, not to mention coaching women entrepreneurs and taking their businesses to the next level.

Then, of course, there is my young son who needs lots of time and attention – we have been doing all kinds of things and I love the warmer weather!

I started working with a new client this week and she was trying to figure out why she could not bring in any new business or clients. I asked her how she was currently marketing her business and she said with Facebook.

Immediately I knew why she wasn't getting any new business. Facebook is an AWESOME tool for marketing your business, however there is a right and wrong way to do it, and most people are doing it wrong. If you are not driving traffic from Facebook onto your own personal list, then you are doing it wrong.

You don't own Facebook and therefore you don't own any of your friends and contacts on Facebook. If they decide to delete your account for any reason, all of your contacts are gone and I know plenty of people it has happened to.

Secondly, when you communicate with anyone online in a place like Facebook, you are talking to them in a space where there are millions of others as well. You should be looking for places to talk to your prospects where other people are not.

How awesome would it be if YOU were the ONLY person communicating with them and eliminating competition? That's why you need to build your own email list fast. I'll talk some more about that after the weekend.

Day 22: Today's Action

Update your social media profiles to ensure they are fresh and interesting.

Day 23: Shopping Lessons

Well Miami was GREAT, as usual. While I was shopping there, I noticed the business owners doing more than usual to attract clients and customers into their shops.

Miami ALWAYS has people working to hustle up others to dine at their restaurants or shop in their stores. They don't just let people walk by; they hire people to actually talk to you and get you to buy from them. Everyone is hustling up business. But this time, I noticed them doing even more, probably in response to the economy which is of course the smart thing to do.

Stores were holding fashion shows using their sales clerks to model and walk the runway IN THE STORE, all in an effort to get customers inside so they could sell them. I thought it was brilliant.

But it also got me to thinking about how little most people do in their own business to bring in customers. You can't just send an email or post your business link on Facebook; that doesn't work.

You MUST have a list of prospects that you can communicate with. Without a list – which is the key to ANY business – you will not get to the level you want. Having a list means you are targeting your ideal market.

Doing anything else means you are out there blindly marketing to anyone, many of who are not interested in what you are offering.

Building your list is an ongoing process that successful entrepreneurs are working on continuously, that is how and why they are making money.

You need to have a system of marketing to people that is well thought out and delivers a clear and concise message that resonates with your target market.

So if you do not have a list for your business that is TARGETED – and you are not bringing in new prospects – then chances are I have just solved your biggest business challenge!

Day 24: Today's Thought

Our greatest glory consists not in never falling,
but in rising every time we fall.
Oliver Goldsmith

Day 25: Adapting Your Routine

I have been on the go more than usual lately so I have had to adjust my workouts.

Sometimes you have days so full that you have to get a workout in any time that you can. Remember, working out is a normal part of your routine, not something extra you can choose not to do (that's how I want you to look at it).

It doesn't matter what weight you are starting from, all that matters is that you start.

Go walking each day if you are just starting out. And if you are a pro at working out, be sure you are always challenging yourself.

Healthy choices aren't just about going to the gym. Next time you go grocery shopping, take note of what you are putting in your basket. When you choose well at the grocery store, you won't even bring junk into the house.

My cousin told me the other day that if she shops on a full stomach she makes good choices at the store, but if she goes shopping while she is hungry she tends to grab junk food!

What little tricks can you use to make healthier choices in your life?

Day 26: Today's Action

Create 12 welcome messages for your autoresponder (or review and redo your existing messages if you have them already).

Day 29: The "Thank You" Surprise

Such a lovely surprise today; I got a beautiful gift in the mail from a lady who'd attended one of my recent events.

At some of my events, I run what I call a "SuperSeat" where I – along with the other HIGHLY intelligent women in the room – help someone solve their business challenge on the spot!

The ladies who get a chance to sit in my SuperSeat are always excited but this one was so pleased that she sent me a LOVELY gift from Nordstrom. Another recently sent me a glowing email about how she did the things we told her and she is already seeing it work! Check out the email I got after she spent just 15 minutes in my SuperSeat:

I had a wonderful time yesterday! Thank you for the great advice!! I've already made the changes to my site and it's working!!! I am super-duper excited about July... you are such a blessing! Thank you very much!

It's wonderful to get that feedback and it makes me realize how much value there is in a simple thank you. Who can you say "Thank you" to today?

Day 30: Today's Thought

Every great dream begins with a dreamer. Always remember, you have within you the strength, the patience, and the passion to reach for the stars to change the world.
Harriet Tubman

Looking Back and Looking Forward

What are the top five things you have learned this month?

1.

2.

3.

4.

5.

What are the top five actions you will take next month?

1.

2.

3.

4.

5.

MONTH 7

Day 1: Getting Unstuck

I was chatting to a lady in the gym today. I could tell she wasn't full of energy but when she started chatting she was telling me that she was frustrated because she really felt STUCK in her life.

Do you ever feel like that? If you do, then what do you do about it? I find that when we feel trapped, we think it is beyond our control to change our circumstances, when in fact we are the ONLY ones who can change our circumstances!

Being stuck is just a state of mind.

- Nobody forces us to stay in a situation that is not ideal
- Nobody makes us stay in a relationship we don't feel good about
- Nobody makes us stay working in a job we don't like
- Nobody makes us stay stuck running our business the wrong way

In reality, we control all of those things and we have the power to do something about them. If you are not happy in a relationship, then leave. If you do not like your job, then quit and find another one. If you are not happy about how your business is going, then invest in yourself, find a coach or mentor and change the face of your business.

Successful entrepreneurs recognize that they control their own destiny. They do not blame other people for their shortcomings or failures. They learn from their mistakes and they regroup and keep pressing on.

The harsh reality is that we are usually our own biggest obstacle in life, coming up with ways to pacify ourselves as to why something is not going our way. Pointing fingers and placing blame in every direction possible except ourselves.

The day we all learn to look at the woman in the mirror, accept her for the great person she is and promise to work on the areas that need work... is the day we realize that the sky is the limit and accept no more excuses.

So today, you are no longer STUCK in anything you don't want to be in. You either choose to become unstuck or you remain where you are, knowing that YOU made that decision and accept full responsibility for the outcome.

Day 2: Today's Thought
The future belongs to those who believe in the beauty of their dreams.
Eleanor Roosevelt

Day 3: This Crippling Fear
I'm heading out to Vegas to attend James Malinchak's four-day event! I'm especially excited because several Superwomen and many of my coaching clients are also going to be there.

Whenever I go to Vegas, I never get a chance to hang out, so maybe, just maybe, I will actually hit the Vegas scene this time!

As I rush out, here's my question for you: Is FEAR crippling you in your business and in your life?

If the answer is yes, you are definitely not alone. Fear is one of the biggest obstacles in life that we have to overcome. As I spend time with my students working through their roadblocks, FEAR rears its ugly head every time.

It seems that fear has been preventing many people from pursuing their dreams or is keeping them stuck and afraid to make leaps in their life and business. THAT in turn is keeping you from profiting the way you should!

My first secret weapon in combating fear is recognizing and acknowledging that it is a natural human emotion that EVERYONE experiences.

- Fear doesn't care how savvy you are.
- Fear doesn't care how many times you have done something.
- Fear doesn't care if you are new or seasoned at what you do.
- Fear doesn't care what race or gender you are.

Once you accept that fear is normal, you will be better equipped to work through it and go on to accomplish your intended goal. Fear of failure is perfectly normal... but should only be short-lived. Let's face it... when stepping out of your comfort zone and doing something new, the possibility of failure always crosses your mind. There are only two possibilities... failure or success.

But the bright side is that the road to success is full of failure! Few people have achieved success without failing along the way. Failure is just a way of showing you what will and will not work so that you can finally get it right.

So in your business – and in your life – do not let a little thing like fear cripple you to the point you never make a move! Never trying is worse than being afraid!

Day 4: Today's Action

Collect five testimonials on video, audio or text and add them to your website.

Day 5: The Wrong Time to Be Humble

So busy here in Vegas but I wanted to share a quick thought. Guess what? Everyone is not going to believe in you, or your purpose and passion. But that isn't your job anyway, so who cares?

Your job as an entrepreneur is to bless the world with your talents that are being used to enrich the lives of other people. If you have a passion that is making money for you as well as helping others reach their potential, or solve their problem, then you are indeed gifting people every day.

Many women have a difficult time tooting their own horns because they were raised to remain humble. Remaining humble and promoting yourself are two different things.

If you have a product or service that is genuinely helping people, then it is your job to extend your services to the world so that you can help even more people... and you can do all that while being humble!

Day 8: Today's Thought

Commitment leads to action. Action brings your dream closer.
Marcia Wieder

Day 9: Making an Impact

I had an awesome time in Vegas at the James Malinchak event! Saw some of the usual suspects and connected with a bunch of brand new people.

I was also excited to see some of my coaching students there; they had a great time and are now bursting with new ideas and concepts.

That is what happens when you network and move in various circles of influence, it can be downright life-changing!

So you want to help as many people as possible? I find that many entrepreneurs have that same mission. Besides running a profitable and lucrative business, their goal in life is to give back to their community, church, children or an organization they are really passionate about.

But keep in mind, no matter how badly you want to carry out your mission, you will be unable to make a difference or impact until you get yourself and your business in the best position possible... and you do that by investing in YOU to learn the proper systems to put in place so that your business is profiting. See, it's not enough to WANT to give back, nothing will happen until you put in the effort to profit so that you can affect the masses.

The last couple of events that I have gone to reminded me of this powerful concept. Besides James Malinchak being an awesome businessman and entrepreneur, he is also a great person who has the same mission as the rest of us... to give back.

Not only does he educate other people on how to make their businesses profitable, but I have seen him raise $50,000, $100,000 and more at his live events for his children's organization. Do you see the power in that?

Close your eyes for a second and imagine that you are having your own live event, with people who have come to learn from you. On top of your great event, you have the power to ask your attendees to help donate and raise money for the charity or group you are passionate about.

Then imagine the joy of being able to write that big check for your organization of choice. How powerful and awesome is that? Not only are you operating an awesome business that is enriching the lives of other people, but you are now also in a place to give back and fulfill your mission in life!

Entrepreneurship obviously has its perks when it is done right! That means working on your business, investing in learning proven systems and being consistent.

Day 10: Today's Action

List five things you can outsource then check out an outsourcing website and find someone to do them.

Day 11: The Wealth Killer

I am home today with my son! The school called and said he got sick, so I am on Superwoman nurse duty! Hopefully it is just a 24-hour bug. But while I am here, I wanted to share some thoughts on a problem that is killing businesses everywhere – PROCRASTINATION!

As I work with my coaching clients, I am amazed at how many of them are being held back due to the lack of discipline. Well, I shouldn't say that I am amazed, it's just that they are looking for something else to be the reason for why they are not profiting to their potential. In fact, many times, it boils down to time management and discipline. And that is ok, because there is an easy fix for it!

As women we STAY busy, juggling many, many jobs; nobody knows that better than me. But there is a way to ensure that you put the time you need into your business so that it can grow and expand and so can your bank account.

It starts with some deep soul-searching and evaluation. As kooky as it sounds, if you just go through this simple exercise, you will uncover the MUCH needed precious time you didn't think existed.

Pay attention to your daily habits.

- How much time are you spending on the phone talking about unimportant things with your friends?
- How much time are you spending on text message conversations about much of nothing?
- How many favorite TV shows do you just HAVE to watch that are sucking precious hours out of your life and taking away from your business?

If you walk around with a journal for a few days and log the hours you are engaging in such activities, you will find the time you swore you didn't have to put into your business to take it to the next level.

What's more important? Your business or the "Housewives?" (Gosh, I love that show!)

Day 12: Today's Thought

A failure is a man who has blundered,
but is not able to cash in on the experience.
Elbert Hubbard

Day 15: What They Really Want

I got a call today from a potential new client who wanted my help to fix a big problem she had.

She'd spent months developing a new product only to discover she couldn't sell it. This is way too common – I often discover people spend time and money creating products and services for their customers only to find out nobody wants them.

I mean, as entrepreneurs, we are serious about helping out our target market; we want to provide them with solutions, right? I bet you put your heart and soul into your product creations, offered them to the world only to realize lackluster sales.

If you've faced a let-down like this which caused you deep pain, grief and money, let me clear something up for you. It's not that your products weren't any good, in fact most likely they were great; it was probably due to something else. Let's try to figure out what went wrong:

1. Perhaps you marketed them to the wrong people. Is your list comprised of people who are interested in what you do? Or do you randomly send emails and offerings to everybody you know – including family and friends who have no confirmed interest? Do you even have a list? (If not you HAVE to get one)

2. Did you create your products without doing the proper research to figure out if there was a desire in your market for them? Did you know for a FACT that what you created was fulfilling a need in your customer base, or did you just assume?

3. Do you have a marketing system and process for your business that is proven to work and that does all the hard work for you, or do you wake up every day on a wild goose chase wondering how you can blindly acquire just one client at a time with no real plan? And most days, nothing is happening.

If you find yourself fitting into any of those categories, truth be told you are FAR from alone. This seems to be the path many entrepreneurs take with their business when they have not received the proper guidance and coaching on what to do and how to do it.

It's a hard, long lesson that unfortunately leads to many people having to close their doors and give up their passions and dreams. But it does NOT have to be that way.

Once you learn how to correct those areas, your business will flourish like everyone else you see and admire. They don't have anything over you, except they learned the right marketing and implementation system. That is EASY to fix!

Day 16: Today's Action

Think about what you would do if you had a whole day free; then schedule a complete day this month to do it – whether it's business or fun.

Day 17: Your Personal Environment

I've just completed redoing the study in my house with the help of my assistant.

She made sure it was warm and cozy and a place where I could be really productive. I cannot believe how small things like colors, candles and comfy chairs have increased my productivity by leaps and bounds.

Working from my new home office is the best thing ever and is definitely one of the things bringing some balance to my life.

I encourage you to do the same. Find a space where you can be productive, feel happy and enjoy a great sense of accomplishment every day.

Even if you need to go out to Target like we did and pick up a couple of things to spruce up your space on a budget, it will make all the difference in the world!

Day 18: Today's Thought

If opportunity doesn't knock, build a door.
Milton Berle

Day 19: Winning Campaigns

The great news this week was that my friend won her campaign to become her State's attorney; I've been working with her on her campaign.

She made history as the first woman to ever hold that position in her county!

Whenever I embark on a new venture (and this was definitely new for me) I make it a point to learn all that I can. I ran the internet marketing for her campaign in an effort to increase her supporters – and raise the money she needed – using the same online techniques I use in my own business and teach to my clients.

I made my candidate add a lot of videos to her list and had to make sure she was "connecting" with her audience. That meant looking directly into the camera and delivering her messages from her heart. Those videos would be her first time addressing people who didn't really know her and I learned a long time ago that connection is key in business.

As I spent this past Tuesday on my feet from 6:45am to 8:00pm (yes, looking for some sympathy) speaking to people at the polls who were coming to vote, I fought the urge to put my sunglasses on. Although the sun was killing my eyes, I knew that wearing sunglasses while trying to sell someone on my candidate was a major mistake.

But as I looked around, other people out lobbying for their candidates had sunglasses on. NO CONNECTION! I even saw many candidates themselves greeting people and asking for their vote with their sunglasses on.

My point is this. Regardless of what media you use in your business, if you are not connecting with your target market, you will NOT win them over and convert them to a client.

It can be Twitter, Facebook, salesletters, TV, radio, it doesn't matter; if you don't find a way to resonate with them, then you are wasting precious time.

My Connection Coach, Jonathan Sprinkles always says this, "If you don't connect, you will NEVER collect." And yes, there are people who teach you how to connect, it IS just that important to your business and sales conversion.

Day 22: Today's Action

Arrange to get a transcription done of the teleseminar you ran (you did do it didn't you?!) Then have the transcript edited to use as a giveaway widget or as a product to sell from your website.

Day 23: Standing Out

Unless you live under a rock, everyone knows we've been experiencing tough economic times. Unfortunately for many, that means they have been suffering in their business, too.

But if you believe for one minute the economy is responsible for your decline in sales, you are in BIG trouble.

I'll say it again... people are still spending money in every single industry out there on whatever they want. They may be tighter with their money than they used to be, but all that means is that they are spending it on the things that are COMPELLING them to whip out their wallets.

Is your product or service compelling? It's your job to make it compelling by learning the right marketing techniques and messages that talk directly to your prospects and clients.

Let me ask you a question. During these tough economic times:

- Did you fire your long time hair stylist and go in search of one who was cheaper?
- Did you stop frequenting your favorite restaurant and go to McDonald's instead?
- Did you stop buying the Christian Dior shoes you love and start shopping at Payless?
- Have you stopped getting your nails done regularly at the salon and started doing them yourself?

For most people the answer to most of those is no!

That is because these are the things in your life that you want and you haven't let the economy stop you from buying them. This pretty much proves my case that people still spend money on whatever they want in ANY economy.

You didn't switch hair stylists because you are too in love with your own to even dare go someplace else. Their services are so good that you couldn't imagine someone else touching your precious hair. And that, my friend is how you should be marketing your own products and services.

If you do NOT have a Unique Selling Proposition (USP) and you don't even know what it is for that matter, it is time to step up your marketing 10-fold.

Your USP is what separates you from your competitors. It is your "hook" and marketing message that makes a person say in absolutely any economy, "I gotta have what you are selling by any means necessary."

Now wouldn't it be great to have people talking about you and your biz that way?

Day 24: Today's Thought

What you do speaks so loudly that I cannot hear what you say.
Ralph Waldo Emerson

Day 25: What Money Is Not

Well here I am in San Diego attending another event with over 400 people in attendance.

I am meeting some awesome entrepreneurs who are living their passion and affecting many lives with their great work. I love investing in products and events; they have helped me immensely in my own business which, in turn, means I have been able to help my own clients in an even BIGGER way.

So, when it matters, do you feel good about what you do? Part of being an entrepreneur is having a genuine interest in affecting the lives of the people you work with.

Your work should allow you to live out your purpose in life, be able to profit from it, and reap the rewards of knowing you are positively making a stamp on the world.

Many people feel "bad" about profiting from their passion, often times because they were raised to think money is evil. Money isn't evil; it's what you choose to do with it that can be good or bad.

If you REALLY want to help people, then the only way you can do that is to help yourself first. The better your own financial position, the bigger your reach because you will have the resources to get your message out BIG!

You have people who need you out there. So if you are a person who has been running your business like a hobby and getting paid like it's a hobby, you can stop that by learning how to ramp up your business so that you profit accordingly!

Money is NOT evil!

Day 26: Today's Action

If you've got kids, talk to them about your business and what you are doing for them.

Day 29: Finding Time

Here I am back home after another great trip to the West Coast.

So here's my question for you today: If somebody has something you want, that you know can make an impact on your life, how far are you willing to go to get it?

Most of my mentors and coaches have events on the West Coast, which is why I spend a lot of time in Las Vegas and in LA. Sure, it's inconvenient for me to take five- hour plane rides and spend three, four or five days in a hotel.

After all, to make that happen, I have to make sure my son is squared away with his school and activities routine while I am gone, my business is in order and a host of other things.

But that is what sacrifice is all about. If somebody can help me increase my business profits or enrich my life in some positive way, I am THERE. And no, I don't sit and wait for them to throw an event in my own backyard because I know that is never going to happen.

People who have knowledge that can affect lives have paid their dues and now they are sharing what they have learned with the world. And if that means I have to endure another long trip to go and get their knowledge, then I am doing it.

Life isn't always convenient and who am I to think that someone who has something I want should pack up and come to me? Actually that is quite ridiculous to even think that way.

Let's face it, we are all busy doing what we do, running around trying to make a bunch of things happen at one time without losing our sanity. But if you are not willing to do what it takes to go and get the knowledge you need, then you can't complain about where you are stuck or falling short; because that is the decision that YOU made.

Most of us need to get to a point where we can stop working IN our business and instead work ON our business to make it grow and expand. And part of that is getting the education to make that happen by any means necessary... even if it isn't always convenient.

It's funny how we can make time for the things we want like vacations and fun, but we always make excuses when we need to carve out time to get serious about our business.

So next time you make excuses about why you can't carve out the time to educate yourself, think about how easily you were able to do it when you wanted to go on vacation. Kinda makes you say hmmmmm, right?

Day 30: Today's Thought

Look well to this day. Yesterday is but a dream and tomorrow but a vision. But today well-lived makes every yesterday a dream of happiness and every tomorrow a vision of hope. Look well therefore to this day.
Francis Gray

Looking Back and Looking Forward

What are the top five things you have learned this month?

1.

2.

3.

4.

5.

What are the top five actions you will take next month?

1.

2.

3.

4.

5.

MONTH 8

Day 1: Grasping Opportunities

I'm sitting here in the airport, about to board my flight to Florida where I will be taping my segment for the Lifetime TV show "The Balancing Act."

I'm super excited that Superwoman Lifestyle was a mission and purpose that even Lifetime Television took notice of!

I remember the first time I got asked to appear on TV. I was terrified, but I wasn't going to miss out on the opportunity.

Have you ever kicked yourself for not following your instincts? For not pursuing an opportunity in life you knew you were destined for? For not pulling back from something or someone you knew was not good for you? Of course you have, we ALL have.

So what are your instincts like in business? Who are you giving into that is preventing you from pursuing your dreams and working full force to make them come to fruition?

Forget about the outside negative forces, the unsupportive partner or all your friends telling you that you are being ridiculous. That negativity will always exist.

I want to focus on the "number" you are doing on yourself, that negative person within your own head that is preventing you from giving 100% to your true purpose and passions.

Here is the truth... if you are NOT uncomfortable, then you are not working hard enough in your business. If you don't wake up with butterflies in your stomach with apprehension and fear about some aspect of your business, you are not working hard enough.

If you are feeling totally comfortable, then you are not working hard enough. Instead you are playing it safe. And when you play it safe as an entrepreneur, it means you are not growing.

Entrepreneurs are risk-takers; we do things the average person wouldn't. We put ourselves out there for the world to criticize, but we keep on moving because we have a bigger mission.

We have gifts and talents and we can affect change and make someone's life richer. But none of that can be done if you are not pushing yourself everyday beyond your comfort zone.

Look at it this way.... if you have amazing talents, products and services that you believe can help enrich someone's life, then why are you holding back from them?

Don't you think it is your time to shine and shine in a BIG way? I do!

Day 2: Today's Thought

To be successful, you have to have your heart in your business, and your business in your heart.
Thomas Watson, Sr.

Day 3: Standing Up for Yourself

I received an email yesterday from someone who had a confession to make. She said that she is sick and tired of giving her friends business advice when she isn't using the advice herself in her own business.

She admitted that she talks a good talk, but at the end of the day, she is guilty of not applying the advice to her own business and quite frankly... she feels like a fraud.

I encouraged her to not be so down on or harsh on herself because she is not the only person living this reality; she was just fed up to the point she was ready to admit it to someone.

So many entrepreneurs know what to do, but have problems doing it. Implementation remains a struggle for many people, but look at it this way... it is better to do it NOW, proactively, before you HAVE to do it because you find yourself in a really tight spot that may be tough to get out of!

Don't let people, time, fear, negativity or self-doubt stop you from living the life you were destined to live and from profiting from your true passions!

Day 4: Today's Action

Decide on the title for the book you want to write to help your business and outline your ideas for the chapters.

Day 5: Stop Killing Yourself

I've just been listening to some women chatting in the grocery store and it seems to me that so many of us feel bad because we compare ourselves with others too much.

If you ever find yourself doing that, I want to tell you something important: Stop killing yourself trying to do what you see someone else doing!

Isn't it crazy how we wish we could be like someone else that we see who "appears" to have it all together? Who appears to be the perfect mom and wife? Who appears to have their business running so well and still be able to get dinner on the table every day at 5:00pm?

Superwoman Lifestyle was created to celebrate and embrace ALL women doing the best they can. We are all different and what may be easy for one person may not work for another.

Don't keep judging and comparing yourself to other women you feel have it going on. Instead, pat yourself on the back for all the strides that you are making to maintain some kind of balance in your life.

And always remember… for every person you admire, there are several more there admiring you as well.

Day 8: Today's Thought

If you work just for money, you'll never make it, but if you love what you're doing and you always put the customer first, success will be yours.
Ray Kroc

Day 9: Following Up

I am sitting here developing some material for the new students of my next coaching program and I thought I would share some of the stuff I will be working on with them.

One point we are going to cover is how to develop a killer "follow-up" marketing campaign to boost your sales by 60 percent!

The key to sales is in the follow up! I am always reminding my subscribers about my events, products and services I am offering.

I honestly don't do it to get on their nerves, I do it because it's a proven fact that most sales happen in the FOLLOW-UP. This is a critical fact that many entrepreneurs just don't get.

You can't market to a person one time and expect them to respond right away. You know that little thing called "Life?" Well life gets in the way for everyone. We have intentions on doing things and taking action but we are easily sidetracked... by the phone, by the kids, by EVERYTHING.

And so in your business, when you are promoting something, you had better be able to design a follow-up campaign or strategy for reminding people about what you are doing. When a person doesn't respond right away, it's not because they aren't interested, it's just because they forgot!

One-shot marketing does not work. If you are afraid of annoying someone by communicating with them more than once, then you are in the wrong business! A person who feels you provide value will stay with you forever. A person who is not interested in what you are doing, saying or offering will opt out of your list.

Don't take it personally, they just weren't your target market anyway and were NEVER going to invest with you. And we only want to direct our messages to people who represent our target market.

So if you are one of the people who are scared to annoy someone, then today I am giving you permission to start multiple communications and stop worrying about it. They either want you and your stuff, or they don't. Period! Okay?

Day 10: Today's Action

Pick something you've done recently that you're happy about and then give yourself a reward – you choose what – for doing it.

Day 11: The Truth About Your Business

Sometimes, when I hear people talk about their businesses, I'm surprised at the statistics saying so many businesses fail.

The way many people talk you would believe their business was truly thriving but the reality, behind the scenes, is they aren't making any money.

So many entrepreneurs are falling into the trap of having their egos stroked. But what are you most interested in doing? Making people think you are doing well or actually filling up your bank account?

With the advent of social media like Facebook and Twitter, people are able to hide behind a computer and pretend to be doing all kinds of things. And because it looks good, most people will actually buy into it. And sure, it feels good to have people on Facebook post all types of great things about you and your business. But, at the end of the day, are ANY of these people actually paying you for your products or services?

Are you sick and tired of people saying how much they love your blog or your teleseminars and webinars... but they never actually invest with you?

If the answer is yes, then you are not alone by a long shot. I have people sending me emails all the time asking my advice on why they can't get people to buy from them. Yes, people may love what you have to say and tell you that you are great, but why aren't they paying you? THAT is the big question!

Typically it is because there is something wrong with your process. Perhaps you are giving away every single thing you know, making the person feel as if they have what they need already. Or maybe you aren't giving enough away, leaving the person feeling like you haven't provided them with any real content.

And maybe you never learned the proper way to construct your teleseminars and live events, and so you are lacking a proven conversion process.

Perhaps you haven't yet learned how to properly write compelling marketing messages. Or, maybe you are talking to the wrong market who can't afford to pay you.

Of course you can fix any of those things, but it starts with being committed to working ON your business and not IN your business. Remember, at the end of the day, you started your business to make money, not impress people. So I ask you, is your business a REAL business, paying you like a business, or are you stuck in the "hobby zone?"

Day 12: Today's Thought

There is time for work, and time for love. That leaves no other time.
Coco Chanel

Day 15: Confusing Your Customers

I received an email from a frustrated woman business owner who feels she is communicating effectively with her list of subscribers, but they are not signing up to work with her or buying her products.

She says that she consistently markets to them and, no matter what, it's just not working. I know how frustrating this can be, but it's just not as simple as most people think.

Yes, step one is to email your list consistently; this she is definitely doing right. But she showed me a couple of examples of the emails she is sending and I was able to immediately identify the problem.

The emails are confusing. She doesn't stick to one brand. In each email, there is a new header and new tag line signifying something different about her business.

These are the things about branding that DO matter a lot. As I always say, cute pictures and headers don't make a person decide to buy from you... you staying consistent on WHO you are and WHAT you do is what helps a person decide you are the one for them.

CONFUSED PEOPLE DO NOT BUY! If you find people always asking exactly what you do and needing clarification, then your positioning in the market is wrong and you are KILLING your business.

Next, your email marketing cannot be all about YOU and what YOU are doing. Focus on providing solutions to your target market and CLEARLY illustrating the great benefits of working with you, and how it will directly and positively impact THEIR lives.

And it always helps to have social proof; people want to see OTHER people singing your praises, rather than you being the only one singing your praises! People want examples of what you have done for others before they invest in you.

Lastly, if you are the one deciding what your market wants and needs, solely based on your own assumptions and opinions, then you are probably missing the mark.

Trying to sell products and services that do not appeal to your market just because YOU think they need it is a fatal mistake. Your job is to find out what your ideal client is craving and wanting. Once they tell you, THEN you go and fulfill that need for them.

There is nothing worse than creating a product you THINK your audience wants only to find out not one person was interested. BIG waste of time and money (been there done that).

People are making thousands and even millions of dollars by learning the art and science of effective email marketing. Simply being articulate and having good grammar is NOT going to cut it. In business, it's all about the psychology behind what makes a person say yes or no to you.

It's a skill set you MUST acquire or you will be sending emails forever that get little to no response from your market and that is no fun!

Day 16: Today's Action

Find a way to package the services you offer differently so you can charge more for them.

Day 17: Breakthroughs

My newest coaching members are having some major breakthroughs in their business and we have only just begun! One person has already picked up a new client by improving her presentation skills and making her "talk" more appealing and clear.

Getting crystal clear and concise in your business is the key to everything else flowing. The other new client is currently getting her webpage in the RIGHT order so that she can go on TV and drive traffic from her appearance. I am super excited about her new life coaching business and the media opportunity that has come her way.

Still another client from the UK had a major breakthrough by realizing her marketing messages were incongruent with the products and services she is offering. Now we are tweaking them to make sure they are just right to increase her business profits, and to get her ready for her live event this summer!

I'm sharing this with you to illustrate the point that there are some key things in your business that MUST be aligned in order for you to profit. Most entrepreneurs I work with have some outstanding products and services, but without the right positioning, marketing and systems... the business won't work at all, or it will barely function.

So if you have been busy doing "busy work" in your business and avoiding fixing the REAL issues that are preventing you from reaching your goals, then today I want you to STOP. Stop and take inventory on where you are putting your time.

- Are you creating products and services without knowing if your market really wants them?

- Are you putting together events and teleseminars that aren't converting anyone to a real paying client?
- Are you spending too much time on social media, but not realizing any monetary gain from it?

If the answer is yes, today I want you breathe and let it go. Evaluate what is going to make money for you and get rid of the things that are just making you "feel" like you are accomplishing something.

Trust me; I have to do it all the time. It's easy to get caught up being busy, but it's better to get caught up making money!

Day 18: Today's Thought

Most of us have trouble juggling. The woman who says she doesn't is someone whom I admire but have never met.
Barbara Walters

Day 19: Get Outside

So here I am in Starbucks having some creative time.

Sometimes it's hard to sit at a desk and work – especially when the weather is nice.

There is this constant struggle to focus on work, yet take some time out to do something enjoyable, even if it's just letting the sun shine on your face, or taking a nice walk with your iPod on.

You can even take your computer with you and go sit outside someplace nice – don't forget to charge your battery. Even doing what I'm doing right now – sitting by the window in Starbucks – can help you get more done.

It's important to shake up your routine sometimes to keep yourself fresh and motivated. Try it, I guarantee you will feel refreshed!

Day 22: Today's Action

Create a detailed 'avatar' of your ideal customer describing in detail what they are like and even give them a name. This will help you serve them better and communicate more effectively with them.

Day 23: First Steps

In this week's issue of my ezine E-volve, I invited readers to submit a question to me about their business challenges. Here's one I received from Gail and my response.

Hi Vicki
I am a Nail Technician and Foot Reflexologist. I have just launched a spot to perform my services in a Salon located in MD. I have found two upscale vegan nail lacquers, but I am having a difficult time trying to get people to switch to a healthier version of nail care with a price of $20 for a manicure.

I am only offering healthy nail alternatives. I need to get someone to help me compose some literature on what my mission is for a healthier nail alternative. I really would like for us to stop going into those toxic nail salons inhaling poison chemicals... what should I do? Where do I start?
Gail

Hi Gail,
Congrats on launching your nail service! My fist piece of advice is to always conduct market research first before you launch any new product or service.

While you obviously have good intentions in trying to steer people towards a healthier solution, you still have to pay attention to what your market says that it wants. What we think as entrepreneurs is good for people and what they need, is not what they necessarily want.

People make buying decisions based on wants rather than needs. So when launching something new, you must first survey your market and see if there is potential interest. It is very difficult to persuade people they need something, but if you give them what they say they actually want, you will win every time.

At this point in time, you must write some compelling marketing messages that clearly outline the benefits of using your product versus what they were using before.

Through artful writing you must be able to "move" people and show them all of the positive outcomes they will experience as a result of using your product. It won't be about YOUR mission, but rather about how it will benefit them. Always remember at the end of the day, all your customers want to know is what is in it for them!

Day 24: Today's Thought

One's feelings waste themselves in words; they ought all to be distilled into actions which bring results.
Florence Nightingale

Day 25: Is This Holding You Back?

I was recently interviewed for an article in a magazine and they asked me what I thought was holding a lot of people back from fulfilling their entrepreneurial desires and making them successful.

I am a firm believer that a few CORE things are a MUST for success in business. A mentor/coach to equip you with the marketing knowledge is a no-brainer, without it, I am 99% sure most people are struggling. But also a weak mind. And when I say a weak mind, I mean allowing the opinions and comments of others to drive your decisions in life and business.

Allowing unqualified people to tell you that your ideas are bad. Not doing what needs to be done simply because you are afraid to fail and, even bigger than that, you are afraid of people laughing at you.

Unless you get to the point of not giving a damn, you will remain a slave to the commentary of random "people." People don't matter when it comes to YOU doing something bigger for the enrichment of yourself and your family. People shouldn't be given the power to rule your life and decisions when they should be more concerned with their own lives.

An entrepreneur on a path to success is immune to criticism. They recognize that jealousy and envy comes with their plight.

- They KNOW that people unhappy with themselves or their own life will have a hard time being happy for them.
- They KNOW they will lose friends who tell them they have "changed."

In actuality, nothing about you has changed except your deep desire to WIN and succeed. But "people" only see that you are doing something they wish they too could do, and unfortunately in comes out in a negative way. OH WELL!

I know PLENTY of people who have put the brakes on their dreams out of fear of losing friends! Trading in your goals and success in order to appease unhappy people is RIDICULOUS! Why? Because they are going to be unhappy whether you are successful or not! It's not your problem.

If you are going to fail, then fail on your own! But do NOT fail because you never tried in order to keep friends. Because guess what? Those are NOT true friends!

Clean house and surround yourself with more positive people who are secure in themselves and have the ability to motivate and encourage you. Those types of people DO exist.

They are like-minded people who also have aspirations. They aren't threatened by you, but rather they are inspired by you!

Day 26: Today's Action

Find a new place to network – either online or offline – that will allow you to reach your ideal customers or business partners.

Day 29: Giving People What They Want

This past weekend we hosted our monthly Metro Money Makers Meeting to a crowd of 300! My husband Lloyd and his business partner Greg Davis showed everyone how he makes up to 50K per day with affiliate marketing, a unique style of internet marketing.

People were blown away; Greg shows real proof of his earnings so people know he is the real deal. I am excited for all the people that joined their new program, that means Lloyd and Greg are about to make even more millionaires and I am always excited to see people work hard and prosper!

What about you? Is everything going well despite the economy or are you feeling frustrated and in danger of giving up? If so, let me assure you of something. Regardless of the economy, there truly are ways to recession proof any business.

Think about this.... people will never stop spending money on the things they want. Did you notice I said WANT and not NEED? As a business owner or entrepreneur, it is your responsibility to give your target audience what they want.

People make buying decisions based on wants. How many times have you allowed things you NEED to suffer because you WANTED something else?

You may need to pay your gas bill, but when it comes down to that new pair of designer shoes that you want, what will the final decision be?

Get my point? So do not design your marketing strategy around your personal perception of what your clients need.

You will not make it doing that. It is your job to talk to them and see what they WANT. Sounds simple, but it a big mistake many people make.

I do not want for you to get caught up in making excuses for your business and blaming it on the economy or recession. That is negative thinking and serves no purpose. Furthermore, you don't have to be a victim of the economy.

How is it that so many businesses are still thriving? It is because those businesses learned how to market effectively so that they are not affected. Everything in business boils down to your ability to attract and retain customers.

Without these core skills, your business can easily fold. I received many, many emails from real estate investing coaches nationally who were amazed at how many women came to my last event in May.

They are now having trouble filling seats in their business and they were blaming it on the economy. Before this recession, they had no problems getting people to come out. But now, they are stalled. I explained that I have the knowledge to switch up my style and business models and messages depending on what is going on in the economy.

Knowing how to tweak your plan is crucial to surviving what many people are viewing as some of our worst economic times. Without this skill, you are risking having to shut your doors. And now is not the time to shut your doors, now is the time to be building multiple streams of income.

Day 30: Today's Thought

A woman with a voice is by definition a strong woman. But the search to find that voice can be remarkably difficult.
Melinda Gates

Looking Back and Looking Forward

What are the top five things you have learned this month?

1.

2.

3.

4.

5.

What are the top five actions you will take next month?

1.

2.

3.

4.

5.

MONTH 9

Day 1: Overcoming Fear

I have a date with my son this afternoon; we are going to the movies!

He doesn't go back to school for a few days and summer camp is over.

That means he is home with me and all I hear all day is "Mommy, mommy, mommy. Mommy, watch this and mommy watch that." You know how it goes! LOL

This is a critical time of year for me, I have a dozen high level Mastermind Members gearing up for my 12-month coaching program. These business owners are invested at a high level with big plans for business reinvention by working closely with me and my team for an entire year.

I also have my small group telecoaching program getting ready to launch for this quarter and we are putting together the latest and greatest business strategies for those attendees as well.

I am extremely excited to be working with so many diverse entrepreneurs and business owners, who are all ready to dive in and make BIG shifts in their business and who are all sick of trying to figure things out on their own.

Not a fun place to be and unfortunately a place that will have you stuck year after year with mounting frustration. I don't want that for anyone!

Anyway, today, one of my email subscribers sent me an email admitting that she has been avoiding focusing on the money-making aspects of her business because quite frankly it scared her!

This person received BIG kudos from me simply because most people will never admit it! She is also sick and tired of people telling her how great she is and how inspirational, but none of these people are paying her. In other words, the compliments and flattery are getting her nowhere!

From working with thousands of people on how to increase their business profits and bottom line, I know first-hand that it is a natural tendency to shy away from sales and marketing. But I also know first-hand that anyone not focusing on sales and marketing is not making money in their business, no matter what they say or what image they try to portray to others.

Women in general have a tendency to focus on "women empowerment" – something I am all for, but only in moderation. The term is extremely over-used, abused and taken out of context. In fact you will probably never hear me say this term.

Here is the reason why... women in business are already empowered and know that they have special gifts to offer the world. They would not have started a business unless they were motivated and believed in their expertise.

Being in the company of like-minded women is a powerful thing when you need a charge or reminder of all that is possible and we all need that from time to time.

However where women empowerment gets dangerous is when women start to believe that is the ONLY education they need. Then they start to attend event after event in search of the next motivational message, thinking that is the key to making their business profits explode.

That is a false sense of security and, as my email subscriber boldly confessed to me, a way of her avoiding having to deal with learning the "hard" skills of making money in her business.

Look at it this way. You can attend a motivational event every day of the week for a year, but it won't give you what you need to keep your business afloat. You can believe in your abilities all you want, but it won't give you what you need to make money in your business.

There is a skill set involved in making money in your business that must be acquired. If you want to learn how to be a doctor you go to medical school. If you want to practice law, you must go to law school. And if you want to run a successful business you must learn the mechanics and skills to make that happen. It's no different.

Do you ever see guys going to "men empowerment" events? Heck no. The guys I see making big money are learning how to market, convert prospects, write copy, and the art of sales... the things they know are needed to reap the financial rewards.

And it's time for women to do the same. So while women empowerment is great for that pick me up, social piece and reminder of what is possible, at the end of the day we still have to learn how to make the big bucks like the big boys!

Don't let another year pass you by where flattery, well wishes and compliments pacify you, I would much rather have you turn those compliments into cash!

Day 2: Today's Thought

I've learned that people will forget what you said, people will forget what you did, but people will never forget how you made them feel.
Maya Angelou

Day 3: When Friends Get in the Way

Have you ever heard that phrase, "make new friends but keep the old; one is silver and the other is gold?"

I remember learning that song when I was in elementary school, my friends and I used to sing it all the time. And like many people, I mistakenly thought that the longer your relationships were in terms of length, that means they were stronger than any new ones you would ever make as you grew older.

I was speaking with a client the other day who was letting me know she was distracted from her work because she had a HUGE fall out with her girlfriend of over 15 years. The way she was talking about the whole debacle made it seem as if they were married! LOL

As women, we value our friendships very much. We love and bond with our hair stylists and use them for therapy, right? If we go to another hairdresser we feel like we are cheating on them!

After listening to my client's devastation it all boiled down to her feeling as if her friend was disloyal.

She went on and on about how much she had done for her and how she was there for her when nobody else in the world was. And now, this person turned on her, betrayed her and showed her "true colors" as she put it.

I felt her pain, I really did. But as much as I felt her pain, as her coach, I needed to put things into perspective for her based on my own experiences in life and how I have drastically changed my views on friendships and relationships in general.

First off, life is life. If you believe for ONE minute that you will never face tough times or devastation you are kidding yourself. NOBODY sails through life without challenges, heart breaks and major let downs. So you had better be prepared!

Second, although loyalty is GREAT and indeed an admirable quality... I'm sorry, but the amount of people who will ever TRULY be loyal to you, you can count on one hand.

Being loyal requires a few things. It requires a person to have conviction. It requires a person to blindly trust and believe in you when others will not. It requires people to have stances that most will be against. It requires a person to go with their gut versus what is popular. And it requires a person who is prepared to suffer consequences with you when nobody else will.

So my point is that no matter how LONG you have been friends or even in a great romantic OR business relationship with someone, you will NEVER know who is loyal to you until that person is tested.

Unfortunately for my client, her friendship was tested 15 years in. THAT is why she is devastated. She believed the longevity of the friendship automatically meant something more than what it really does.

Have you ever had someone come into your life who is practically a stranger that ended up holding you down beyond your wildest dreams? Or perhaps they did something for you that your own family would have never done? There is your proof that it is not about the length of the relationship, but rather the heart and soul of the person.

So the next time you put your EVERYTHING into your relationships, remember that you will NEVER know who is really silver and who is really gold until they pass the test!

Day 4: Today's Action

Find a commitment buddy – someone that will keep on top of you and make sure you get things done. You can do the same for them.

Day 5: Spiderwebbing

I just got back from meeting my son Lloyd's teacher; he starts a new school soon. I'm getting a little sad as I look at his long legs and see how much he is growing up. ALMOST makes me want to have another baby, but then I quickly snap out of it! LOL

So back to business! Do you know where your prospects and clients are coming from? What are you doing to be seen EVERYWHERE?

Those two questions are extremely important to your business for a couple of reasons. One, it lets you know what media you are using to market that is working well, and two, knowing that allows you to concentrate your marketing in areas that are working and pull back from those that are not. This will save you both time and money.

As for making sure you are EVERYWHERE; that, too, is critical to your business. You must diversify your marketing efforts and be sure to cover a wide range of places you are seen. Anyone relying on one sole method of marketing their business – like social media - is most likely not getting the results they anticipated.

Successful business owners are using a variety of ways to get their message out to the world. My mentor James Malinchak refers to this strategy as "spiderwebbing." Using this term allows you to get a visual and see how casting your marketing web in a variety of places can bring prospects and clients back to your funnel from different avenues.

You should be speaking on other people's stages, using social media, using your website and having traffic driven to it, attending seminars and events, radio, TV, magazine interviews, radio interviews, writing books and giving interviews!

Here is a perfect example. I was on a consultation call yesterday with someone who wanted to inquire about coaching with me. I asked her immediately how she heard about me. Guess what she said? She said she saw me in Millionaire Blueprint Magazine with my husband years ago! WOW. I think that was in like 2007!

Then she said she has seen me in promotions and videos with other top marketers and that she sees me hanging out with James Malinchak and other successful people. She wants to be associated with people who are in those circles too.

This illustrates the importance of being EVERYWHERE! If this person first heard of me in 2007, here we are six years later and she is on the phone with me and ready to work with me now!

It's not by coincidence that this happens, it is by design. There is no reason in the world why you too can't employ this strategy for your business and bring in droves of potential clients from a variety of different places.

It is your job as an entrepreneur to spread your message wide and far so that you can experience the ultimate business success you so deserve and help the people your product or service was designed to help.

So today, I want you to go out and cast your marketing web!

Day 8: Today's Thought

Throw your dreams into space like a kite, and you do not know what it will bring back, a new life, a new friend, a new love, a new country.
Anais Nin

155

Day 9: Always a Marketer

There are so many amazing things going on for my clients! Books are being completed, major media deals are being inked and business has never been better!

Yes, even in an economy like the one in recent years, entrepreneurs are having their best years ever, simply because they have invested in learning how to consistently bring in new business, and market themselves.

I always tell my clients: as soon as you realize you are a marketer and make that mind-shift your business will see the results.

Every single entrepreneur or business owner must accept that they are a marketer and must make it a priority!

Day 10: Today's Action

Contact a diet or food expert to discuss your diet and see if you are eating food that is harming your energy or your health.

Day 11: Email Marketing

I am smack dab in the middle of several different coaching programs for entrepreneurs who are on a mission to design a profitable business.

One emerging issue coming up consistently is the frustration people are experiencing trying to master the art of "email marketing." Sound familiar?

There aren't too many businesses today that can't be marketed and promoted online! In fact if you are NOT marketing your business online, I can guarantee you aren't making anywhere near the money you could be making. After all, online marketing is the new Yellow Pages.

But the challenge people are facing is how to get someone online to purchase their products and services. Once a person is on your list, just what do you say to convince them that your product is PERFECT for them? Once a person listens to your amazing teleclass, what do you say to get them to want to work with you even more?

The answer is simple! You must learn HOW to speak to your target market! You must learn what their issues and problems are so that you can write to those points and show people that you understand their desires. You also must be able to connect with people and make them like you! Nobody does business with people they do not like.

And if you are not connecting with people and establishing a rapport with them, then there is no way they can get to know and like you either.

I get that this is an area people struggle in. Writer's block prevents you from thinking of things to say and write about; then, before you know it, you are no longer communicating with your list on a regular basis. This inconsistency is a list killer, a trust breaker and something you NEVER want to do.

When you spend precious time and money building up a qualified list of prospects, the LAST thing you want to do is make them lose interest by not delivering what you say you will.

Day 12: Today's Thought

Whatever you do, be different – that was the advice my mother gave me, and I can't think of better advice for an entrepreneur. If you're different, you will stand out.
Anita Roddick

Day 15: Making It On Your Own

Someone sent me an email saying they no longer wanted to be on my list because they didn't need any help and they made it "ON THEIR OWN!" She used all caps, just like that! I was like WOW, really? LOL

Here is the deal. I personally don't know too many people who made it on their own. Every successful person I know, had help from someone else, and I know a lot of successful people very well.

Even the success stories we see on TV of famous people, when they tell their story, they speak of someone in their life who mentored them or coached them and pushed them.

So point blank, this woman was lying. Why? Because most likely she is in denial. In denial about her business and unwilling to accept help from anyone because she is so busy "pretending" she has made it. I have seen this pattern before and it saddens me because it forces people into a corner they don't know how to get out of.

We have all heard of faking it until you make it, right? Well some people take the faking a bit too far. Have you ever seen someone you KNOW on Facebook or Twitter bragging about how much money they made or all these grand things they are doing, when in reality you know that is not their life?

I see it all the time. I am sitting there like, "Really, Really?" You owe your own momma money and everybody else I know and you are bold face lying on social media!

Well guess what? That is happening all day every day. And for some people the lies about their business success (and personal life) have spiraled so far out of control, they don't know what to do anymore, so they just keep on telling more lies.

The problem with this is that the practice of keeping up this façade has become a fulltime job when in reality behind the scenes the business is not booming, money is not coming in and you are in a bad situation all around. But there is no time to REALLY work on the business because you are too preoccupied with your social media deception.

I see deadbeat dads pretending to be great dads with great careers when they owe thousands in child support, I see people in horrible marriages pretending they are in marital bliss, all kinds of foolery!

Let's face it! None of us are perfect and we all have struggles and bad times. We all have shortcomings and things we need to work on. That is life and that is being human. And being able to admit that will set you free!

Instead of trying to "make it on your own" simply because you don't want people to have a real glimpse of what your life is really like, understand that you are not alone. We are ALL jacked up in some way, but so what! Find someone you know can help you get the tools you need and invest in you, your most important asset!

I want you to accept who you are and where you are in life and business right now, and then design a plan to improve it. THAT is what is most important. Nobody jumps on the scene with instant success; there is a road to travel and a foundation to build in order to get there.

Day 16: Today's Action

Spend the day at a spa.

Day 17: Using an Ezine

I've just pressed "send" on my Ezine for this week. It takes a bit of work but it's my favorite way to keep in touch with my subscribers.

How about you? Are you even using Ezines to build rapport with your prospects and clients?

Ezines are online newsletters and I send my E-volve Ezine each week to provide my subscribers with great content and valuable tips and strategies to help boost their business.

At the same time, I am building a relationship with them so they get to know and trust me and see if I can offer any value to them and their business.

I have been faithfully pumping out my E-volve Ezine for about two years now and I have been blogging since 2006. That's a hint that it works in business! For me to be writing since 2006 means something good is going on, right?

Ezines are often times your first point of contact with new prospects who want to check you out and see what you are all about. Yes, it's very similar to dating! You go slow in the beginning of the relationship and test the waters. If you like him, you like him and continue on, but if not you cut it off.

I have a client who told me she gets upset when people "opt out" from her Ezine. I told her that is a part of business and not everyone will stay engaged and find value in what she does and that is perfectly ok. The only people you should even want on your list are those who are serious about their business and fully engaged.

For the serious person who finds your communications beneficial, they will be eagerly waiting for anything you put out and introduce them to. That is your target market and who you are in search of to help with your product or service.

If you take inventory, you will see that the real movers and shakers in the world of entrepreneurship are using Ezines and similar communication vehicles to stay in touch with their prospects and clients. It is THE catalyst for a long term relationship and something EVERYONE should be doing.

Not only that, but please do it consistently. If you offer someone a weekly Ezine when they sign up on your list, please don't be sporadic and only send it once a month or when you remember.

If you fall into that trap, you have lost trust with your list immediately and it will most likely be too late to save the relationship.

Don't be noncommittal like a lot of men; say what you are going to do and DO IT! LOL.

Day 18: Today's Thought

Perseverance is failing nineteen times and succeeding the twentieth.
Julie Andrews

Day 19: Explaining My Mantra

In a recent interview I had with Essence.com, the writer wanted me to explain my mantra, Business, Beauty and Balance. She particularly wanted me to explain the "Beauty" part.

As women, when we have to perform or present either in the board room or in our own live events, we need to feel good about how we look.

When we are having an "off" day and feeling self-conscious for whatever reason, it shows up in our work. We can't concentrate. Know the feeling?

So in teaching the whole Superwoman Lifestyle to women in business, I stress taking time to make sure you feel good about how you look and feel in mind, body and soul. How great does it feel to strut into the room with all eyes on you knowing you look great?

On the flip side, how awful does it feel to walk in with all eyes on you and be preoccupied with your appearance to the point you can't be your best?

So yes, making sure you take the time to feel good about YOU from head to toe is crucial! Never neglect yourself; you are far too important!

Day 22: Today's Action

Get someone to interview you, record the interview, then have it transcribed and turn it into a giveaway widget or a product you can sell.

Day 23: The Right Mindset

On the road again! I am on my way to a big marketing conference in Chicago for entrepreneurs and business owners. I'm conducting a roundtable session there and my topic will be on "Unique Branding for Increased Media Opportunities."

I am super excited for the opportunity to teach my expertise to thousands of entrepreneurs!

Speaking of media opportunities, I just did a story for The Investor's Business Daily where they wanted to know all about my own big annual event and how I put it together. What an honor – and great publicity as well.

Your ability to attract opportunity and create a successful business is first and foremost rooted in your belief system. One of the questions I am frequently asked is "what does it take to truly build and run a great business as an entrepreneur?"

The answer is not as profound as you may think it would be.

Your mindset has to be right first. If you believe self-investment is paying for something, then you are sinking your ship before you even get started.

People with a wealthy and healthy mindset focus on investment versus payment. When you invest in something, you are putting something in to get something way greater in return out.

Picture this. Would you give me $100 if I gave you $500 back? Of course you would, you would do that all day long!

When you invest in learning ways to better yourself and your business, you do so knowing that what you learn will bring you a positive return. Knowing just one new strategy or concept can forever change the face of your business.

On the flip side, so many of us have been raised to invest in things that don't bring any return at all. Investing in designer clothes and shoes and fancy vacations don't bring you any return on investment.

In fact they put you further in debt! But sadly enough, this way of thinking is all too prevalent and one of the biggest reasons women in business aren't further along.

I'm going to give you a real example. A client of mine invested in my recent one-day Reinvention Retreat. I worked with her on a new business model, strategy and income stream for her business.

She took what she learned and only two weeks later, not only did she recoup the investment she made with me, but she is profiting from this new business model. Just that ONE idea, changed the face of her business in only two weeks. Not too shabby, huh?

That very reason is why I and other entrepreneurs continue to invest. We profit from it, plain and simple!

So take a moment and think about what mindset you are in. If it's not wealthy and healthy, then you MUST work on it in order to progress!

Day 24: Today's Thought

A lot of people are afraid to say what they want. That's why they don't get what they want.
Madonna

Day 25: Hope Marketing

I was holding a training call with some of my Mastermind coaching clients last night along with a special guest who shared some multi-million dollar strategies with us that were mind-blowing!

Things got really good when we started talking about "Hope Marketing."

Hope marketing is basically putting your product out there and hoping someone buys it from you. Doesn't sound too powerful does it? That's because it's not!

Promotion of your business, product or service requires some very deliberate action on your part. There are a series of things you need to do in order to get anyone to buy from you.

Simply saying, "hey, look what I have" is not going to cut it. If you have tried this approach before, I am certain you know exactly what I am talking about.

The steps and actions you need to take to successfully make sales in your business are built in strategy, marketing "know how", and the psychology behind WHAT exactly makes a person say YES!

Today, I want to share a few of them with you, just so you can take an assessment and see if you are using ANY of them, or if you need to start jumping on this right away:

1. Know EXACTLY who your target market is; talking to the wrong people is a huge waste of time. This has to be done through market research, surveys and getting in tune with your people. And of course people who cannot afford your price points are NOT your market; you have to find the people who can.

2. When you have something to sell, make sure you let people know in advance about it to help create buzz and anticipation.

This is done with an effective product launch campaign both online and in many cases offline marketing, meaning good old fashioned MAIL.

3. Knowing WHAT to say and HOW to say it through effective copywriting and the use of compelling copy.

4. If you market, promote and sell your services online, NOT knowing how to write emails that move people towards the action you want them to take is the #1 reason why most people don't buy from you. You haven't done a good job of making them feel they need it and that can only be accomplished through your copy.

HINT: Effective copywriting does NOT mean good grammar and big fancy words, it means being able to show the benefits of your product or service and connecting with your market's WANTS and desires, and solving their problems.

So how do you rate? Are you doing any of these things? Have you invested in learning any of these strategies? Or do you need to start doing something NEW?

Day 26: Today's Action
Call an old friend just to say hello.

Day 29: Getting Paid What You Are Worth

One of the top frustrations I hear from my clients is that people are constantly asking them to lower their prices or even give them their stuff for free with promises of payment later.

RUN quickly from this. If you value what you do and you have invested time and energy into your expertise, then you should value yourself enough not to waver on your fees.

If you are having a hard time closing people and getting them to invest in your services, it may be because you are talking to the wrong people!

No matter how great your product or service is, if the person can't afford your prices, it's like trying to squeeze blood from a turnip, ain't gonna happen!

The RIGHT people are those who fit within the right demographic as far as income levels needed to invest with you. That is why doing market research and getting laser focused on WHO your target market really is remains one of the most important steps you must take in your business!

While we all want to help people, the fact of the matter is that if people know they can "bargain" with you they will do it every time. And once you lower your standards in business it is hard to bring them back up. I used to try and "help" people, too, and wound up burned most of the time. I realized that I wasn't being respected and I was harming myself.

It wasn't until I charged what I was worth that I saw the laws of reciprocity turn in my favor.

You are your most important asset in your business. Always invest in yourself, treat yourself well, demand what you are worth and watch the profit tides turn in your favor!

Always remember you DESERVE to be compensated for your amazing gifts and expertise!

Day 30: Today's Thought

How wonderful it is that nobody need wait a single moment before starting to improve the world.
Anne Frank

Looking Back and Looking Forward

What are the top five things you have learned this month?

1.

2.

3.

4.

5.

What are the top five actions you will take next month?

1.

2.

3.

4.

5.

MONTH 10

Day 1: Doing Something for You

Exactly what have you done for YOURSELF lately? I am getting concerned about the many women who are confessing to how burnt out they feel.

Women are going through their days with a smile on their face appearing to have it all together, but behind the scenes quietly suffering. After speaking with several women, here is what I am finding; I wonder if this sounds familiar to you...

Perhaps you are gauging and judging yourself against your best friend who makes running her business and managing her family look like a breeze.

Or maybe you think you aren't measuring up to your neighbor who runs through the neighborhood jogging while pushing her baby in the stroller. And maybe you feel like you aren't progressing enough in your business because at the end of the day you haven't accomplished the 10 things you put on your action list and you feel let down and deflated.

This is what I call Superwoman Envy! I created the Superwoman Lifestyle movement to celebrate women everywhere.

There are people who will tell you to let go of the whole Superwoman mentality, but I say EMBRACE it. Let's be real, as women we are born nurturers and we will never stop multi-tasking, it's pretty much impossible.

So instead of trying to buck what is a natural inclination, here is what you should do...

Define what being a Superwoman means to YOU! Don't worry about your friends and neighbors and what they are doing, define "having it all" for yourself. We are all different and the dynamics of our lives are different from everyone else.

If you can't accomplish 10 things each day in your business or life, then make that a more attainable goal of two or three things.

That way, each day when you lay your head down to sleep, you will feel good knowing you moved a minimum of 1% towards your goals and you accomplished something.

The sooner we as women stop comparing ourselves to other people, the better off we will be and it's at that time that we give ourselves permission to embrace our own strengths.

Day 2: Today's Thought

You only live once but if you do it right, once is enough.
Mae West

Day 3: You Are Not Perfect

Nobody is perfect and to expect someone to be perfect is unrealistic. I don't care how much you admire someone for their looks, their clothes or their business savvy, they too are making mistakes in life.

To some extent, we are all a product of our upbringing and our past.

Some of us were raised by loving parents who instilled great values and some of us were not. Some of us never had positive role models in life.

Some people never even had parents and were raised by someone else, or in the foster care system perhaps.

Some of us long for the father we never had or someone just to say "I love you," or "I am so proud of you."

However, whatever environment you were raised in, it doesn't have to define you for the rest of your life.

I work with women all of the time who carry the weight and baggage from a not so great past or upbringing that they allow to haunt them in every aspect of their life.

I have also seen some women who came from some horrible circumstances that have gone on to give so much value back to the world through sharing their experiences and gifts.

These women have acknowledged their past but also proven that it does not have to define who you go on to be.

If you are a person who makes a mistake and learns from it, then kudos to you. If you are a person who continues to make the same mistakes over and over again, then you have some serious self-reflection to do.

When you know better, you CAN do better.

When you know better and you REFUSE to do better, you need to ask yourself why you are continuing to punish yourself with self-sabotage when the whole world can see that you are indeed worthy!

Day 4: Today's Action

Choose one new way to drive traffic to your website and focus on that for the next two weeks.

Day 5: Shiny New Syndrome

Okay, so yes I am out of town again, this time in sunny LA attending another fabulous networking and training event.

Just before I left, I had to have a heart to heart talk with one of my clients! She told me she didn't mind if I shared our conversation if it could help just one person who has fallen into this "trap."

She has the "Shiny New Syndrome" disease! The shiny new syndrome disease is when you hop from thing to thing, event to event and course to course.

Women with this syndrome love to invest in themselves and attend events and sign up for courses. But the problem is that they never really implement in their business. Not only that, but they overwhelm themselves with so much information and each idea gets grander than the next.

Doing this is sure to keep you stuck for a couple of reasons. One because you never sit down and implement the basics in your business. The basics represent the foundation we all need to get a business structure in place that is going to work for us.

Second, this syndrome keeps you in a whirlwind where you are constantly changing your business name, mission and branding which is keeping your audience confused and quite frankly causing them to lose trust in you.

When they see you doing this, they assume you are still "finding yourself" and no longer feel confident you can help them because you yourself do not appear to be established.

Enough about the devastating effects of this entrepreneurial disease, let's find a solution! First make the commitment to yourself to not get caught up in all the hype in business; most of it is just a pile of distracting junk.

You must stick to the core things that the most successful people are doing, the people with a proven track record.

Second, ask yourself if you are floundering because you are avoiding the implementation phase of your business. I know that implementation is the biggest roadblock for people in business and so what happens is that you end up avoiding it by jumping from thing to thing.

You keep yourself busy doing busy work but, when you look up, not much is being accomplished and the money you deserve to be making is not being made.

Day 8: Today's Thought

In all realms of life it takes courage to stretch your limits, express your power, and fulfill your potential.
Suze Orman

Day 9: Making Connections

So now I'm back home after another great event where I learned some amazing content and new strategies. I will definitely be implementing them into my own business as well as passing on to my own event attendees and clients!

But it wasn't all work; I got a chance to attend the Prince concert with Chante Moore and my good friend Cheryl, her manager! Chante got on stage with Prince and jammed out and I caught Sheila E's drum stick! Needless to say, it was an amazing night and the Superwomen were in full force!

Connection is definitely key! Let me ask you a question... are you finding ways to connect with influential people who could make a difference in your life and business? If not, you are making a HUGE mistake!

We can't run a successful business alone, we need coaches and mentors to show us the right way, this theory has been proven over and over again. Likewise we need to connect with other people who can introduce us to key players and open up the doors of opportunity.

One great line I take from the event in LA I just attended was "your income will not increase until your Circle of Influence increases."

Now this doesn't mean that you should be running up to key people asking them to invest in your products and services, that is a SURE way to run your name in the ground. It means that you should be offering key players something of value and offering to be of service to them first. It's not about taking from people; it's about giving and serving.

When I was in LA, several people introduced themselves to me and let me know they came to the event because they were on my list and heard me talking about how great it was.

They also mentioned all of the great value they gleaned from my weekly E-volve Ezine. That is pretty powerful, don't you think?

Through serving people and giving them great content, they hopped on a plane and flew to LA just based on what I said, and never met me before. It is for this reason that standing out and networking the RIGHT way should be on the top of your priority list.

So let me ask you... what is the last networking event you attended? And even more importantly, when you attended the event did you talk to key players or did you stay on the wall? Hmmmmm!

Day 10: Today's Action

Choose a reward that you will give yourself when you complete a task you are currently working on.

Day 11: Buying Decisions

So after attending someone else's great event last weekend, I'm excited to discover that my own next event is filled to capacity!

I'm really motivated for it because there is nothing better than seeing lives and businesses reinvented for maximum profit!

The fact of the matter is that most people already have great businesses and concepts; the problem is in the lack of systems, unique positioning in the market place and not knowing HOW to talk to your target market.

Nothing a little makeover can't fix!

Did you know that what you say and how you say it directly affects the buying decision of your prospects? If you are not in tune with their desires, problems and wants, then you will be unable to deliver powerful messages that resonate with them.

Think about how YOU make your own buying decisions. You act when a message really talks to you and makes you feel as if the product or service were created for you. Almost like they knew exactly what was going on in your head. THAT is what moves a person to invest with you.

But if you never take the time to learn the hot buttons and problems of your prospects, you will not be equipped to effectively communicate with them, thus losing the sale.

It's not your job to assume you know what your market needs. People do not make buying decisions on needs, they make them on wants.

The correct way is to let your market tell YOU what they want and then you provide that solution for them. Doing it the other way is a big waste of time and money, trust me I have tried.

Take some time to survey your list and see what is going on with them (I hope you have a list). Oftentimes they will let you know exactly what they are craving so that you can provide it for them instead of playing the assumption game!

Day 12: Today's Thought

It matters not what someone is born, but what they grow to be.
J. K. Rowling

Day 15: Finding the Right Partner

I had an amazing weekend at the UFC fights in DC on Saturday! Both of my husband's fighters won and we had a HUGE after party celebrating my husband Lloyd's 15 year anniversary for his martial arts school. It was also my girls' weekend with my best buddies from high school and they are now fight fans!

So is it me or does it seem like everyone is partnering up these days?

Partnerships can be a good thing... or they can be a bad thing, depending on who you go into partnership with.

Speaking from direct experience, I can tell you some of the pitfalls to avoid when trying to decide who to partner with! I have had my own horror stories and have heard horror stories from my clients and coaching students that will make your skin crawl.

Can you believe I even had a partner one time who hid the fact he had a full-time government job for YEARS and pretended to be a full-time entrepreneur? After I spoke to others who worked with him, the trail of lies was a mile long and this was a pattern of behavior. Crazy, right?

You will be amazed the lengths dishonest people will go to in order to create an appearance about themselves that is far from the truth!

You must always protect yourself and your business! Here are some key things to beware of and some things to think about when you are considering a partnership of any kind in your business:

- I find that many people partner with others simply because they are afraid to go into business alone and want the security of someone else being "in it" with them. BAD IDEA, partnerships should never be made out of fear, this is NOT a good reason.
- Only partner with people who bring something to the relationship. For instance if one person has the money to fund the business, but the other has the marketing knowledge to make it work, that is a partnership where each person is bringing something extremely valuable to the business. This makes sense.
- Never partner with someone who has nothing of value to bring to the business; for them it is a winning situation because they will benefit from you, but for you, it's a lose/lose situation.
- Never be persuaded by someone who talks the talk, only partner with people who can PROVE their business savvy, success, experience etc. Someone's word is just not good enough; we all know that talk is very cheap!
- Be sure your visions and missions are in alignment and the expected outcomes of the partnership are laid out on paper. There is nothing worse than partners in business not being on the same page; it causes confusion, dissention and ultimately will lead to a nasty split.

People begin partnerships with good intentions, but so many of them go bad if you don't do your research. Bad partnerships have landed plenty of people in court spending big money and wasting valuable time.

So if you are considering a partnership, be sure to follow these guidelines. And if you are in a partnership that you know isn't working due to some of these reasons, then it is time to GET OUT before things get too messy!

Day 16: Today's Action

Spend an hour at a bookstore reading the magazines to conduct market research, learn from the headlines they use and identify topical issues.

Day 17: Networking Secrets

I'm just heading out to a friend's book signing. I'm super excited for her because I remember the event to launch my own first book and there is something special about becoming an "author."

I had a super invitation-only official book signing party at a nice swanky place.

Of course tonight's event will be fabulous for networking but... did you know that most people do not know the proper way to network?

Networking is not just attending random events and passing out business cards. It's about establishing relationships and attending the RIGHT events.

Here is what most people do. They attend networking events with the sole purpose of landing a new client and passing out as many business cards as possible in hopes people will buy whatever their product or service is. NOT GOOD!

The first thing to be mindful of is the actual event you are attending. Are the people who will be coming out even your target market, or are you just hoping? Are the people coming out established with a proven track record in business? Are they movers and shakers?

These questions are important because networking takes time, and you want to be sure the event you are attending will be worth your time.

Second, never go out with the intentions of it being all about you. Self-serving tactics are easily picked up on by others. The better thing to do is to come from a place of service and see how YOU can benefit or help someone else. Sounds simple, right? But most don't do it.

Hopefully, when you meet people, you don't make it all strictly about business; people connect with each other by finding out they have mutual personal interests. That is why so many deals are made on the golf course. I can't tell you how many major deals have been made simply by each person loving the game!

The savvy networker is looking to get to know people and build long lasting relationships that are mutually beneficial. Showing your value and worth is important, but showing your integrity and desire to help others is even more important.

And you definitely don't want to be one of those people who invite someone out for a meeting and you don't even pick up the check! That is not good and is a major deal-killer.

Always remember that people do business with people they get to know, like and trust. If you have not yet mastered the game of proper networking, it's time to step up your game!

Day 18: Today's Thought
A man is not a financial plan
Kim Kiyosaki

Day 19: Implementation
I am calling on my Superwoman Powers this week! I am super busy trying to get as much work done as possible before I head out to Vegas for my wedding anniversary and my husband's big UFC fight.

We are the MAIN event at the MGM GRAND and we have invited all of our internet marketing buddies to come hang out, mastermind and celebrate with us.

My big live event is right around the corner and we are busy plugging away to make this THE event for serious women in business. It's no secret that I am all about the marketing is it?

I can't help it, I am on a mission to teach women the REAL "how to make money" skills and get them focused on what generates income like the big boys do it!

I had to take a moment to reflect on how grateful I am to be able to expose women to some of the top entrepreneurs in the business today.

Our speakers and guests are self-made people like you and I who left their jobs to realize their dreams and impact the world with their gifts. Not only that, but the willingness to give back to others and give them the blueprints to how they did it, step by step.

For those ladies coming to the Extreme Women Entrepreneurs event, I had to issue a warning. As my mentor James Malinchak says, "the information, blueprints and strategies you will be handed only work when YOU put them to action."

Implementation is hard for a lot of people – and 10 times harder when you don't run your business on a system or know how to bring in new prospects and convert them to customers.

Waking up every day wondering what to do next in your business is no fun. Not knowing where your next client or sale will come from is even worse. That is not a business... that is a hobby.

Nothing makes me happier than to see someone move from what I call "the hobby phase" to operating and growing a real sustainable business. It's a brand new world!!!

Day 22: Today's Action

Eat what you like today and don't worry about
how many calories it has!

Day 23: Discipline and Commitment

I had a great time at my friend's book signing last week.

One thing that really struck me was how many people said they wished they could write a book. Of course, the fact that so few people do it is the reason why being an author gives you so much credibility.

But, the truth is, it's not that difficult. All it takes is some discipline and commitment!

And those are things that most people struggle with. Lacking discipline and commitment kills our personal goals, kills our business goals and kills our spirit!

Since the beginning of time, we have struggled with doing what is good for us. It's easy to do what is not so good for us, but so hard to do what is most beneficial.

Why is that d'ya think? How does our brain allow us to justify wasteful spending that puts us in debt, but at the same time talks us out of investing in ourselves to learn the things that can take us up a level?

For many people, it has to do with how we were raised. If we were never given examples of self-investment or taught the importance of it, most likely that carries over to adulthood.

Even still, that isn't much of an excuse. At some point we all have to stop blaming our upbringing and poor habits on other people, after all we are in control now and when you know better you do better.

And when you know better but still choose NOT to do better, well then the blame only lies on you!

Every day that you wake up, you are either winning or losing and it's a choice. Every day when you wake up you either choose to be ordinary or you choose to be extraordinary and that too is a choice.

Every day that you wake up and complain about where you are stuck, but never make a move to fix it is yet another choice and conscious decision you have made.

So today you need to make some decisions!

Do you want to be known as one of those people who "talks" about what they want and what they know they should be doing or do you want to be known as one of those people who actually takes action and practices self-discipline?

Day 24: Today's Thought

You have to be open–minded when those early opportunities present themselves; take advantage of them whether they're going to make you a lot of money or not.

Rachael Ray

Day 25: Answering Questions

I've mentioned before that I sometimes invite my ezine readers to submit questions to me with their business challenges. Today I'm sharing another of those emails and my reply:

I am in awe of how much I see you doing! Every time I turn around, it appears as if you are launching a new program or product, or throwing a live event, not to mention I know you have a young son and have a family to tend to. I just want to know how the heck you do it all and if you can provide any tips on how to balance my life so that I don't pull my hair out! - Karen

Hi Karen! GREAT question and one that I know we all struggle with. Let me start by saying that I started my whole Superwoman Lifestyle movement for this exact reason. Women face so many roadblocks when trying to build and grow their businesses and still taking care of themselves, their families and all other competing demands.

Here is what I learned through lots of trial and error. I can only be me and play upon my own personal strengths and the dynamic of MY life.

I think we, as women, have to stop looking at other women we see and wishing we were more like them. If we constantly measure ourselves against people who are totally different from us, we will make ourselves insane.

Living a Superwoman Lifestyle is a mindset and is about YOU defining what that means to you based on your own goals in Business, Beauty and Balance. As long as you are moving a minimum of 1% each day towards your goals in these areas, you can rest easy knowing you gave the needed attention to all things that are important to you in YOUR life.

It doesn't matter if your best friend is able to accomplish six things on her list each day; that is HER. If you are able to knock out three things and feel good about it, then that is good enough!

Once you define and create that space for yourself, you will set yourself free and give yourself permission to move forward in all areas of your life.

Always remember that, for every woman you admire out there, there are ten women looking at and admiring you!

Day 26: Today's Action

Make contact with five past clients or old contacts just to see how they are getting on and find out if there's anything you can do to help them.

Day 29: Making Connections

I'm here in sunny LA on a mini-vacation to celebrate my good friend Cheryl's birthday with some friends. It was hard to fit this trip in with my schedule, but my girl Chante Moore wouldn't STOP pressing me until I committed to coming, so here I am!

After a long but productive week working with my new Mastermind students, my brain is about to pop, so this is right on time. I may as well enjoy it while it lasts because I am planning ANOTHER one of my signature Business Reinvention Retreats and helping even more entrepreneurs set their business up on real systems designed for profit.

These one-day intensives are life changers for people because they come to IMPLEMENT with me and leave with their systems set up, their challenges resolved and ready for profit.

So, did you know that your ability to connect with your prospects can make or break their decision to work with you? Yup, you would be surprised what the reasons that people decide to work with you are based on.

Most people think that people decide to work with them based on qualifications, or their number of years of experience, when in reality often times it is based on how they feel about you.

People decide to invest with people they feel "get them" – which basically means you understand their issues, challenges and problems. If you cannot demonstrate that you get what they are going through, they will not connect with you. You will just be another person offering them services.

Failure to connect with your prospects is often due to your desire to always appear professional, totally put together and perfect in all you do! NOBODY WANTS THAT, lol!

Many times we do this because we take the corporate, 9-5 professional mentality and try to fit that into the world of entrepreneurship, but that doesn't fly here, two totally different worlds!

The person who portrays themself as perfect is doing a couple of things. One, they are pretending they have no problems – which people don't believe anyway. And two, you are putting yourself on a pedestal that will make others feel is unattainable and "out of their league." And that is something that people tend to shy away from.

The BETTER thing to do is be authentic! We are ALL jacked up in some way or another and that is human. People want to know that you are human and make mistakes just like them.

You accomplish this human element by infusing some personality into your marketing. Talk about your dog or cat or kids. Talk about the things you have done that haven't worked so well and the mistakes you have made in business and in life. And let's face it, that gives ALL of us plenty to talk about, now doesn't it? And it also gives people stories to connect with you on.

The moment a prospect says "hmmm that sounds like me too" is the moment they have connected with you and also the moment they decide you are the person for them.

So instead of portraying yourself as a Perfect Patty all of the time, open up and let the more authentic you come out, and watch the response you get from people!

Day 30: Today's Thought

You've got to get up every morning with determination if you're going to go to bed with satisfaction.
George Lorimer

Looking Back and Looking Forward

What are the top five things you have learned this month?

1.

2.

3.

4.

5.

What are the top five actions you will take next month?

1.

2.

3.

4.

5.

MONTH 11

Day 1: Becoming First Choice

I hear entrepreneurs complain all the time that they KNOW they are not charging enough for their products and/or services but they are scared if they raise them, nobody will work with them.

I get it. This is one of those tough hurdles in business that is hard to get over – the fear of scaring people away. The justification that some money is better than no money at all... even when it's not worth your time and it is devaluing your expertise.

Sound familiar? Of course it does!! How do I know? Because it's one of the hardest things for me to get my clients to do.

Here's the deal. You have a gift or talent. You have invested in your craft and you KNOW your stuff works. You solve problems for people. You care about what you do and you put time and thought into it. So why in the world would you practically give it away?

Come with me on a mind-shift real quick. Here is an analogy that I LOVE to use...

You have been going to the same hair stylist for years and you simply love him or her. They care for your hair, they know how to cut it just right and they always leave you looking FIERCE. So one day they tell you that they are going up on their prices because they haven't done so in years and it is time. What do you do?

Do you get upset and decide to go elsewhere and gamble on someone new? Or do you begin paying the new price? Nine out of 10 people will stick with their beloved stylist and pay the new rate! See, they raised their prices and YOU didn't go anywhere, now did you?

Of course not! Here is why... they do an amazing job, they have established a relationship and connection with you – most likely serving as a therapist to all your problems too – and the thought of someone new playing in your hair and messing it up makes you cringe, right? So your stylist has established their value in your life and it has become a "must have" for you.

Well, why can't you think of your OWN products and services the same way? Don't you, too, provide value? Don't you, too, have a connection with your clients? Have you, too, become a MUST HAVE in their lives?

If so, I want you to begin charging what you are truly worth! You never want to be the cheapest in town, people don't want cheap they actually want value!

So if you know you are short-changing yourself, I challenge you to make a change today. Charge what you are worth and target the people who can afford your services! An immediate increase in price is immediate new revenue!

Day 2: Today's Thought

Insanity is doing the same thing over and over again and expecting different results.
Albert Einstein

Day 3: Entrepreneurial Marriages

I've just been reading an amazing book by my great friend the relationship expert Dr. Patty Ann Tublin. She gifted me a copy recently and I wanted to share some of it with you.

She knows all too well how Business, Beauty & Balance all at the same time can be a major challenge!

We as women are often not supported in our endeavors by our spouses or partners. More relationships have been broken due to the many misunderstandings that come from being ambitious in life and business.

If this is YOU, or someone else you know, have them check out Patty's new book, "Not Tonight Dear, I've Got a Business to Run!" The book gives you the tools you need to create a life and business you deserve! Here is a quick excerpt from her book:

"Your relationships with your spouse and children are directly impacted when you take on the challenges of entrepreneurship and/or self-employment.

Unanticipated financial, time and emotional stressors will influence your relationship with your spouse and children and jeopardize your chance for entrepreneurial success if you fail to create a family plan which anticipates the most likely challenges of self-employment.

Married entrepreneurial wives and mothers do not have to sacrifice success in business in order to be happily married and an effective parent!"

Day 4: Today's Action

Book yourself to attend a seminar of live event where you can meet people like you.

Day 5: Paying Attention

I'm heading out to a Red Carpet event in Vegas with my husband Lloyd, and then on to an event in LA with James Malinchak.

I was trying to bypass the red carpet event but my husband and James ganged up on me and told me a REAL Superwoman could swing both! I suggested they both split the cost of a private jet for me. Never heard a peep from them since! Hmmmmm! LOL

Anyway, today I received an email from a young lady who admitted that no matter how hard she tried to stay disciplined and work on her business goals and tasks each day, she ends up falling short.

She wanted to know if I thought something was wrong with her and even questioned if she had an attention deficit disorder, it was THAT serious to her.

The fact of the matter is this. Regardless if you have a bonafide diagnosis of an attention disorder, to some extent we ALL have it. This "thing" called life can get hectic and pull us in a million directions. At the end of the day, you can look up and wonder just where all the time went and realize you haven't done much of anything.

Even the most disciplined person you know has problems staying motivated and focused, that's just the way it is. So what we need to do as entrepreneurs is come up with some strategies to help us stay on target. The tips I am about to give you come from my own experiences as well as the habits of some of the most successful people in the world, including my own mentors.

First thing is first and I hope you don't take this the wrong way... you are NOT smarter than everyone else! When we see successful people doing certain things, for some odd reason we think we don't need to do them or that we can shortcut that process somehow. HUGE MISTAKE!

Cutting corners and ignoring the obvious will keep you stuck in the same place with little to no progress year after year until you grasp some basic concepts. Here are the most glaring success traits that I see run rampant with the people really doing it BIG and doing it WELL:

1. You MUST have a coach or mentor, you can't do it alone, IMPOSSIBLE.
2. You MUST have goals and a plan to reach the goals, keeping them in your head doesn't work, write them down!
3. You MUST assign yourself specific tasks to complete each day and make sure they are REALISTIC! Do NOT let anything take you off course.
4. You MUST stay in the company of other goal-oriented people who "get it."
5. You MUST cut off negative people who whine and complain about their life.
6. You MUST become an avid marketer for your business and learn how to gain clients/customers (without them you don't have a business).
7. You must learn how to take fast action and seize opportunity.
8. Do NOT become a seminar or information junkie who never applies or implements what they learn... Education without implementation is PURELY entertainment.
9. You must be able to envision something greater for yourself, if you can't see it, you probably will never do it.
10. You must NEVER allow fear to prevent you from trying something new. Although fear will never go away, you have to learn to push through it, after-all we ALL have fear and you are not alone.

So take a moment to review this list and put a check next to the things you KNOW you can do better. BE HONEST, nobody is looking but you!

If you find that these are some of the very things stopping you from reaching the level you wish to be at, then it's time to do something new.

191

Always remember that, when you know better, you will do better!!

Day 8: Today's Thought

The only place where success comes before work is in the dictionary.
Vince Lombardi

Day 9: Celebrating Others' Success

What an amazing few days in Vegas and LA. I always come back from these occasions really pumped up to do even more.

You know, I can't help noticing that, lately, I have seen some of the most positive, uplifting people I know have some amazing things happen to them in both life and business!

Every time I hear of their good news, I get so happy; but I am also not surprised at their blessings!

I am often asked what the keys to success are, and although I don't have or know the perfect formula, I do know common traits, patterns, rituals and habits of successful people that remain fairly constant.

One such trait and success principle is the decision to live one's life in a positive mode.

Being positive or negative is a decision that a person makes every single day.

I don't care what has happened, how horrible of an experience one may have gone through, at the end of the day you have a choice – a choice to move forward in a better space or a choice to let the negative person on your shoulder win.

We all know stories of people who have lost limbs in war, been born with abnormalities that put them at a disadvantage, or people who have lost their lives to cancer.

And every last one of them remained a positive person throughout their entire ordeal. Inspiring and giving motivation to others.

These people had a choice, too, and many would say a real reason to be negative, but they decided to go the other way. Quite admirable!

My observations though working with clients over the years is that so much talent is lost and so much potential never realized due to the negativity winning over! And I find that a true shame.

Some people who are surrounded by negativity and raised by negative people have a REALLY hard time breaking the cycle. They have bigger dreams for themselves and some even go for it, but their progress is halted or stalled because they can't shake the old habits.

Habits are hard to break, I know. But if you truly want something greater for yourself and your business, I challenge you to take inventory of the people you associate with.

Do you hang out with people who gossip? Do you hang out with people who are petty in their conversation? People who look to create drama?

Because if you do hang with people like that, nine times out of ten, you are participating in the same negative behavior; the laws of attraction are powerful.

So do yourself a favor if this has hit a nerve with you. Make the decision to move your circle to one of positivity. Whenever you feel yourself getting ready to create drama, tear someone else down or spend your time complaining... I want you to STOP!

Brush the negative person off your shoulder and start over. They say it takes 21 days to break a habit. Imagine the blessings that will open up for yourself, your business and your life! And you deserve that.

Many people have successfully broken this cycle and they will tell you that living positive is a much better life!

Day 10: Today's Action
Find a Mastermind to join.

Day 11: Times Are Better Than You Think

A good friend of mine just called to tell me she'd been laid off from her job. From my own experience as an HR professional, I know only too well that people are always walking into work scared that they will be getting the horrible news that their job is being eliminated.

That is just the reality of the times we have been living in for some time and that will continue to be the case even as the economy improves.

But here's the thing. As I look at my own business and speak to other entrepreneurs, they are actually thriving.

People do not stop spending money in tough economic times but their spending habits and decision making processes do change.

People are not as frivolous with their disposable income but they will continue to spend their money on something. If that "something" is going to be your product or service it's entirely up to you and how you market.

Start by asking yourself a few questions:

- What makes your product or service unique from your competition?
- What are you doing different from them?
- How can you market that uniqueness to distinguish yourself?

Whatever the answer is, that needs to become your "thing" that you market around.

Second, how are you delivering your marketing message? Are you sending a bunch of random people information on your services who may not even be interested? Or are you doing the right thing and marketing to people who are interested in what you have to offer?

If your marketing is not targeted, it is a waste of time and money.

So go out and build a qualified list of prospects who have a genuine interest in your services; that is how you make money and generate income.

Does your marketing have strategic well thought-out multiple campaign steps? Or are you just delivering your marketing message one time and assuming the prospect is not interested if they do not buy?

It is a fact that people normally do not buy the first time. It takes at least five to seven attempts and marketing messages to get someone to buy; so having well-written campaigns steps with great messages that incite people to buy is a must. If you do not have a marketing funnel, then you are in serious trouble.

Are you overlooking your current clients? It is easier to get existing clients to buy from you again than it is to go out and get brand new ones. Why? Because you already have a relationship with them and they trust you. If you continue to deliver great products they will buy from you time and time again. So don't forget them, you are losing out big time if you do!

Day 12: Today's Thought

Successful people are always looking for opportunities to help others. Unsuccessful people are asking, "What's in it for me?"
Brian Tracy

Day 15: Amazing Women Doing Big Things

I've just been invited to take part in the Ms. Biz television show with a panel of women entrepreneurs telling their secrets on what it takes to be successful in business.

It's recorded with a live audience so it will be an exciting chance to meet some amazing women doing big things.

You know doing what others won't do is what sets you apart in life and in business. So many people claim to want to be successful in life, but rarely do their actions match.

I always say that not having your mindset in the right place is a MAJOR problem for most entrepreneurs and those aspiring. If it were super easy, we would all be experiencing major success. But because it takes dedication and sacrifice, few will ever reach that point.

Sacrifice comes at a price, I know. But you have to weigh the odds on your ultimate goals. To be an Olympic champion, you have to train and push your mind and body beyond limits you could ever imagine. That's why there are so few Olympians.

To be successful as an entrepreneur you have to discipline yourself, invest in yourself and stay consistent, but most can't do it.

Example: This summer I would have LOVED to take a vacation, but I couldn't find the time. I had coaching students and obligations in my business that literally had my entire summer booked up.

I held my annual event the day after my wedding anniversary and didn't even see my husband because he was in Vegas coaching his people. Now the average person would have freaked out over the anniversary separation, but it wasn't a blip on our radar.

Why? Because we are both on missions to help others and we realize we can celebrate on another day. Not a big deal.

I had ONE day a couple of weeks ago to take our son to Disneyland, and I had to break up the day to deliver a 3-hour webinar in my hotel room. Most people would have never done that. But I did. After my webinar, we went back out to the park, no big deal.

I have a complimentary call I am giving this Sunday on Building Your Brand, and guess what? I will be in VA Beach with my husband's family, but slipping out for an hour to deliver this call (and he won't even be there because he has a four-day event he is doing).

Again, most people would not do that. But to ME... it's no big deal.

We all have choices in life. You can do what is ordinary and the status quo, or you can begin to take massive actions that set you apart so that you can reach your ultimate goals.

Sure people will call you crazy, talk about you behind your back and even try to bring you down, but that too is another sign that you are moving away from ordinary and starting to dabble into being extraordinary!

Now go and take some MASSIVE RADICAL ACTION in your business!

Day 16: Today's Action

Cut out alcohol or coffee for a week and see how different you feel.

Day 17: Fit, Fine and...

Fit, Fine and Sold Out? Whoo hoo...

I'm super excited! The last couple of years have been dedicated to me stepping up my health and fitness game and my hard work finally paid off!

I am honored to be featured TWICE in FitFigures Magazine for a segment called, Fit, Fine, & Forty.

I was a little reluctant to reveal my age, but when they put it like this, how could I resist? LOL.

Just as in fitness, success in business requires a bit of sacrifice! It means doing things that make people say, "You must be crazy!" It means giving up a lot of what society places value on and deciding what is valuable to you.

It requires you to leave some people behind, even when it hurts. It means sticking to your path regardless of the naysayers.

So many women are struggling in their businesses because they refuse to invest in learning how to attract clients. But they don't know that is the reason they are struggling. So what happens is every other month they are switching gears and trying to come up with something new to make money... new branding, new slogans, new concepts. But none of that will fix the problem.

But the truth of the matter is this... it doesn't matter what business you are in, if you do not learn the money making strategies that keep a business going, it will fail regardless.

If you are not hanging around like-minded motivated people, most likely you are not as motivated as you should be. If you are not networking with other entrepreneurs, most likely you are spending time in circles where entrepreneurship is a foreign concept and probably even ridiculed.

We all are self-motivated to a POINT, but let's face it... there will reach a time when you burn out. And if there is nobody there to hold you accountable or force you to show up, then you are going to suffer a set-back.

Truth is nobody can do this entrepreneurship thing alone. You need allies, you need mentors and coaches and you need accountability.

You need to be challenged and you need to be cheered on.

If any of these key components are missing from your life, it won't matter how good you are at what you do... you will remain stagnant.

Honesty moment here... what is missing from your life or business that is keeping you stuck?

I'm almost certain it is one of the above. FIX IT! I want to see you WIN!

Day 18: Today's Thought
Act as if it were impossible to fail.
Dorothea Brande

Day 19: What Makes a Brand

I had some great questions last night on a teleclass on branding. I could tell some people are getting frustrated and sick and tired of sitting on the sidelines watching people do EXACTLY the same thing they are doing experiencing enormous success!

The people doing what you do however, don't have much over you except proper and profitable branding!

I know many, many people talk about branding all the time, but rarely do they get it right! That's because branding is NOT what most people think it is!

You can't have a logo designed, come up with a great cute and catchy business name and tagline and expect for that to be your brand. That is NOT a brand.

A brand is all about proper positioning in the market place, in fact people could not care less what your logo looks like; they are more interested in what your solutions can do to solve their problems that your competition can't do.

I have personally created TWO successful and profitable brands that have earned me over a million dollars after learning what proper branding and positioning are REALLY about.

Am I saying this to brag? Of course not, I am saying it to show you that HOW you position yourself and your business can make all the difference in the world to your bottom line profit and ability to make people choose YOU over your competition.

So instead of getting frustrated, do something about it!

Day 22: Today's Action
Set aside a family day this month and consider making it regular.

Day 23: Being a Team Player

I have been going a bit bonkers lately! My husband is in Vegas filming a UFC reality show. Translation, I am picking up the slack with him gone and he is pretty much gone for a few weeks.

I'm happy he is on national TV living out his dreams but I do have my moments when I want to fly down there and drag him back on a plane! LOL.

But I am going to be a team player because my time to go and film for TV will be coming soon and I am going to need the same reciprocity! I know how to play the game, trust me!

Do you watch Tabatha's Salon Take Over? Great show, where Tabatha goes into fledgling hair salons and tries to save their businesses!

Her first course of action is to observe and make an assessment of just where the problem resides. Normally it's poor customer service, lack of effective management, and most importantly, A LACK OF EFFECTIVE MARKETING! Like I always say, you can open up whatever business you want, but if you can't bring in the clients and customers, it won't last too long!

Do you ever notice that you will see a new business go up, but walk back by in about 6 months and see a "going out of business" sign?

Same issue. People are under the false assumption that getting a store front, a business license and a website are all you need and that customers will come flocking to you. Unfortunately, it's just not that simple!

The same concept applies for an online business regardless if you are a coach, consultant, speaker or trainer.

No matter how much you try to avoid it, client attraction is king in truly profiting in your business!

I put together a basic checklist to help you determine if you are on the right path, or if you may be heading for that dreaded "going out of business" sign yourself!

1. Do you have a website that captures email?
2. Is traffic being driven to your website?
3. Do you create new products for your business frequently?
4. Do you have a structure in place to move people into higher levels of working with you?
5. Do you have a loyal following of prospects that you consistently communicate with and provide value to?
6. Do people meet you and say, "Hey, I have heard of you before?" (brand recognition)
7. Do you create "buzz" around everything you do?
8. Are you confusing people by changing your brand as often as you change your socks?
9. Do people often ask you what it is exactly you do because they are confused?
10. Are you consistent in all you do or do you work in SPURTS?

Ideally you want all of these things in place, but we all have areas we need to work on. The key is to jump in the game and realize you must run your business on a system and stop treating it like a hobby.

Your challenge is to take inventory of which of these areas you need to bring up to par, and most importantly, actually take action to correct them.

Knowing is half the battle, but DOING is where the money is made!

Day 24: Today's Thought
If you think education is expensive, try ignorance.
Derek Bok

Day 25: Are You Coachable?

I just had a stern talking to with one of my Mastermind members. She has this amazing business, a bunch of ideas floating around in her head and major drive and passion. Her only downfall is insisting on doing it her way. In the end, she had a major breakthrough and is well on her way now!

When you invest with a coach or mentor, I am assuming you do it because you value their knowledge and expertise as well as see them practicing exactly what they preach. You believe they have a blueprint they can give to you to plug into your own business and help get you to the next level.

The next step in making it all work is in being "COACHABLE." Being coachable means that you listen, acknowledge and implement. What it doesn't mean is that you listen, disregard and insist on doing it your way.

Ya see, your way isn't working which is why you made the decision to work with a coach in the first place, right? You must help people to help you, and you do that by trusting the process.

202

No matter how great or talented any coach or mentor is, ultimately the results are up to the student because they must still employ all they have learned and be willing to move forward from practices that don't work.

Being coachable also means making sure you take advice from qualified people. Not your friend, not your graphic designer and not the mailman. Your friend is your friend, your graphic designer is good at graphics and the mailman is great at delivering the mail. But if you are taking advice from them on subjects they have no experience or success in, you are barking up the wrong tree and severely damaging your business.

When I ran my own big event recently, I was joined by two people I consider my mentors. Having them there watching me was added pressure, but it also forced me to step up my game.

In the end, I still got handed a laundry list of things I could do better or improve upon and guess what? I took that list and made the changes immediately. I didn't question, argue or disregard the advice, I took it with pleasure because these mentors have attained levels of success that I admire and respect and any opportunity to get their opinion is one I am all over!

So if you are one of the people who need to work on being coachable, then make sure you think about making that leap. There is always going to be someone who knows more than you, is more successful than you, and is making more money than you. Rather than go against them, JOIN them and watch how easily you too can build an even better business!

Day 26: Today's Action

Give something a complete makeover – whether it's you, your website or your office – you choose.

Day 29: Email Power

I was talking to some fellow entrepreneurs this morning at a networking meeting and it often surprises me how few of them know about or use autoresponders.

As a result, they are missing out on the many benefits in promoting their business. This is definitely one opportunity in your business you don't want to waste.

There are savvy entrepreneurs online who have understood the benefits of having a mailing list, as well as the follow up autoresponder. Once properly put in place, you should see an immediate increase in your profits.

Usually, your customers will take five "touches" to finally decide whether to buy your products or services offered online or not.

The first step in that process is collecting contact details of website visitors. Your autoresponder provider will give you some code to add to your website to help you collect the details.

The next requirement is that you should have good follow up. That's where you use your autoresponder to set up a series of friendly emails to help them get to know you.

Many people are scared off by the technology but they are really easy to operate and have huge benefits in helping you building trust and rapport with prospects.

When you start to build trust, you have the chance to pitch your products or services to your target customers.

An autoresponder is one of the key tools that will help you build a sustainable business.

Day 30: Today's Thought

*It is only when we truly know and understand that we have a
limited time on Earth and that we have no way of knowing when our
time is up that we will begin to live each day to the fullest,
as if it were the only one we had.*
Elisabeth Kubler-Ross

Looking Back and Looking Forward

What are the top five things you have learned this month?

1.

2.

3.

4.

5.

What are the top five actions you will take next month?

1.

2.

3.

4.

5.

MONTH 12

Day 1: Not Giving In

I am so honored to have hosted a room full of women in business – and those aspiring – this past weekend at my own event.

To have so many people sacrifice and dedicate three days to you because they believe in your message is something I am truly grateful for and do not take lightly.

Based on the feedback I received, it seems I did my job on over-delivering and everyone was blown away! Glad to know that, I try very hard to give it my all!

I've run several of these successful events now and one of the highlights of them for me was being able to introduce people to Stedman Graham.

While we all know him as Oprah's boyfriend, many people do not know that he has been running an extremely successful consulting firm for over 15 years. He teaches major corporations on topics ranging from diversity and leadership to branding your business.

One of the most profound things that stood out for me when he spoke is not allowing your past to define who you are today. He spoke of negativity and how people can smell it a mile away when someone gives off that vibe.

A person who grew up in a negative environment has a very hard time letting go as an adult. If someone constantly put you down and told you that you would never amount to anything then, after a while, you begin to believe it.

I know many people who, try as hard as they may, cannot shake the negative person on their shoulder sabotaging their own progress – as well as those around them. A person like this HAS to be called out in order to effectively make a change.

The reason I say this is because they don't realize they are doing it because it has become a way of life. And, if everybody allows them to get away with it, they will never have to face the behavior for what it is.

It's hard to tell someone something about themselves without having specific examples to give them, so when the negativity occurs, address it right away. We all have "things" to overcome in life and we are all a work in progress.

But we can only begin to work on those things when they are addressed; we don't run from them, and we resolve to become better people.

So please do not let your past or anyone else define you! You have to stay in control of who you ultimately wish to become!

Day 2: Today's Thought

You were born to win, but to be a winner, you must plan to win, prepare to win, and expect to win.

Zig Ziglar

Day 3: Making Family a Priority

Is your family all over the place? Do your kids all have their own schedule of activities? Do you find yourself dropping off kids to all types of practices and not having time to even cook dinner?

I know how hectic it can get.

But we have got to find a way to bring everyone together to just enjoy. My husband's schedule is such that my son and I have to have dinner alone. But we sit down together and I ask him about his day at school.

On the weekends, I love to do an activity with my family and have that sacred time. Sometimes we even get together with friends with kids and bring everyone together that way.

In a day and time with so much technology, it is easy for everyone to go their separate ways.

Nothing beats the time and attention we can devote to family; it has to be a priority in life. Just another challenge of the Superwoman!

Day 4: Today's Action

Give yourself some more time – unsubscribe from email lists that don't give you value.

Day 5: Special Projects

I'm at an amazing resort outside of Las Vegas that I never even knew existed! I am here to work on a special project I will be rolling out in a few months, as well as a chance to mix and mingle with a small group of really smart entrepreneurs!

One of the top things I see derailing the progress and success of women entrepreneurs is their lack of focus!

Every other week they are rebranding their brand, talking about something new, and taking on new unrelated projects.

Why? Because it's easier to start something new than to complete something in totality!

As entrepreneurs, many of us are creative, right? And although creativity is a gift, it can also be our downfall.

We can barely sleep at night thinking about the next BIG thing we want to do in our business.

The ideas just keep on coming and we can't shut the brain off no matter how hard we try!

Here is the issue... when we do this, people can clearly see that we are all over the place. We begin to cause confusion and make people wonder just how stable we really are.

The LAST thing you ever want to do in business is have people look at you and your marketing and say, "what the heck is she doing now?" And trust me that is what they are saying.

See, your potential clients are looking for someone who has it all together because they probably do not. They are looking for someone with a solid plan of action to help them solve their problems and solutions.

And if YOU are offering those solutions, but portray the appearance of hopping from thing to thing, then you are turning people off!

I know it's hard to stay focused on your mission, but for the sake of your business you must stick to the core things that generate income.

Cute and shiny new things rarely produce results. Stick to the basics that are tried and true and don't get lured away no matter how sexy that big idea may be!

Day 8: Today's Thought

The secret of getting ahead is getting started.
Sally Berger

Day 9: Positive Circles

I read an amazing article from my friend MaryEllen today! She went in pretty hard on people who only have negative comments when it comes to the success of other people. Yup, it's jealousy rearing its ugly head again!

It bothers me when I hear women tearing other women down. First of all, rarely is anyone an overnight success. There is blood, sweat and tears involved in attaining any level of success, but just because you don't see them doesn't mean they don't exist. That's the stuff behind the curtain.

A successful person is working to make it happen. They are investing in themselves to get the tools they need to move forward and surviving the bumps in the road we all have to take.

Instead of tearing that down, it is to be celebrated. Instead of focusing on their success in a negative way, it's much better to see what they did and pick up some tips and strategies that you too can use.

I personally LUV meeting successful women and admire so many of them. I am always reaching out and offering my assistance to help others. I connect people all the time in hopes they can do business together and help serve with their gifts and expertise.

My friend MaryEllen Tribby has built THREE multi-million dollar companies and she offered to help me in any way she can.

When I sat down for lunch with her, I wasn't jealous of her success, I was amazed and excited to be able to learn from her and very grateful for the opportunity, as she is FIERCE!

You never know what path someone had to take to get where they are.

It's ok to envy what someone else has; I do it all the time. Envy means you want it for yourself, but you are also happy for the person who has it. That is a source of motivation to work harder and it's a good thing.

But for the people who bombard you with the negativity just because they can't be happy for someone else, it's time to step away and find a more positive circle.

Day 10: Today's Action

Schedule a complete working day this month to take off and do what you want.

Day 11: Connecting with People Who've Done It

Yesterday I had an amazing VIP day at my house with one of my Platinum Millionaire Mastermind Members.

We were kicking off our strategy to take her business to the level it could and should be, and what we will be working on over the course of the next 12 months together.

Whenever I sit down with my coaching members, one of the first things that I do is to have them tell me what they have been doing that is working and what they have been doing that is not working.

She confessed to some major frustration when it came to networking events that I am starting to hear from people more and more.

You will always hear people tell you to "get out there and network" but few people really know how to network the RIGHT way or the right networking events to attend.

First and foremost, many networking events are being put on by people who have no real purpose or goal for the event; it's just kind of a cool thing to do. Bringing people together for refreshments and to pass out business cards is not an effective networking event.

You should be attending events where the people add some kind of business value. There should be people there with knowledge and expertise that you do not have so that you can connect with them. The people in attendance should have a proven track record of doing what they say they can do.

A networking event that is full of people who are all struggling to make their business work is not a good use of your time. You want to move in circles of people who are experiencing success, not who are struggling, too. How can people who are all struggling help each other? They can't.

The wiser thing to do is connect with people who have been there, done that and can prove it. People are starting businesses claiming to be able to help other people when they themselves are floundering in their own business. I don't think that is fair or ethical, and certain to catch up to them one day.

If you are attending events where everyone is coming in hopes of scoring a new client, the chances are slim to none that is happening.

But if you attend the RIGHT events with the goal of providing value to others and coming from a place of service and reciprocity, then the tides and karma are likely to change in your favor.

You should always value your time and think very carefully how you use it.

If you have been on the networking circuit and see no positive monetary gain from it, it may be time to do something new or find the RIGHT events with the RIGHT people.

You don't ask your attorney for medical advice, and you don't ask your doctor about the law. The same applies for your business, make sure you are connecting with people who REALLY know – through a proven track record – what they are talking about; not just talking the talk with no social proof. People are getting sick of that.

So if you too have been logging in many hours and sacrificing much of your time on the networking scene with nothing to show for it, I hope these tips will help steer you in the right direction. There are some great ones out there, make sure you find them!

Day 12: Today's Thought

Nobody cares if you can't dance well. Just get up and dance. Great dancers are not great because of their technique; they are great because of their passion.
Martha Graham

Day 15: Finding Customers Who Can Afford You

One of the challenges faced by many of my clients and entrepreneurs in general is deciding how to price their products and services. People seem to be torn between charging what they are worth and not wanting to "spook" people by appearing too highly priced.

Before you can even set prices for your product or service, you must first take a look at your competitors and see what they have going on. Looking at what other people in your industry or niche are doing helps to give you a starting point for making this big decision.

What you will find is that your competitors will fall into three basic categories. Highest, medium and lowest.

Let me start by saying you NEVER want to be the lowest priced. It sends a message to people that you don't value what you do and perhaps you don't think you are worth it.

Additionally, it is very difficult to see a substantial return on investment when you set your prices low; in some cases you may be going in the red. Time is money, and your time is valuable.

Being placed in the medium category is better, as long as you are able to turn a profit and you are not working with little to show for it.

But being in the highest place or close to it is ideal. It conveys that you are a leading authority in your area and that you deeply value the transformation you are able to bring to your client or customers.

Couple of things to be aware of:

1. You can't place yourself in the highest category without providing social proof of people you have provided value to. Social proof and having rave reviews from people you have worked with helps to establish your expertise and solidify your place in your field. What other people have to say about you is ten times more powerful than anything you can ever say about yourself.

2. Additionally you can't place yourself in the highest level unless you too are investing in YOURSELF at a high level. It's incongruent and something that people will notice right away.

Regardless of where you decide to set your prices, one thing is certain. If you lack the confidence to state your prices without wavering, people will see that and will choose not to work with you.

You must feel good about your worth and confident marketing your business to the world.

If you entertain conversations of bartering services or reducing your prices to accommodate everyone who wants to work with you, you are single-handedly killing your credibility and your business.

If you are finding that you are CONSISTENTLY being asked to reduce your prices, the problem is very clear. You are talking to and marketing to the WRONG people. Your ideal client is one who can afford to pay you, not the ones who can't.

When we go to the store and can't afford the Jimmy Choo shoes, we can't pick up the phone and ask Mr. Choo to reduce the price or give us a hook up, now can we? And you should run your business the same way!

It's a simple fix when you learn how to find the RIGHT people, and how to attract them to you. Once again it all goes back to your ability to effectively market using a proven system that works for you on autopilot.

Don't waste any more time bartering with people or reducing your prices, FIX this glaring problem that is preventing you from making the money you deserve!

If you don't value yourself, how can you expect someone else to?

Day 16: Today's Action

Get to know the finances of your business so you know where you are making money and where you are wasting it.

Day 17: Are You Getting Paid to Speak

I work with a lot of different people, from all industries and niches, one of them being speakers. I find that many people are passionate about sharing their story with the world in hopes it will inspire and motivate people to take action and better their lives.

What I have also found is that there are two categories of speakers. Those that are speaking and not getting paid for it, and those that command high fees to speak.

Whenever I work with any of my personal clients that are speakers, one of the first things I ask them is if they are getting paid a fee to speak.

Alarmingly, I am finding that so many people are not getting paid at all! They are hopping on airplanes, spending money for hotels and jumping on stages without a thing to show for it!

This bothers me for a few reasons. One, because I am all about you running your business like a business and NOT like a hobby. If you are agreeing to speak for people and not charging, then you are doing yourself a huge disservice.

Are there ever exceptions? Of course there are. Sometimes you will speak for a benefit or charity event and that is both amazing and commendable.

And sometimes you will speak because you are able to sell your product or service from the stage in front of your TARGET market, and that too is a win/win situation because you can make money from your back of the room sales.

But if organizations that are profiting from their event are asking you to speak without paying you and you are not selling from the stage, then you are once again treating your business like a hobby and allowing others to do the same.

The speakers who are REALLY speakers are getting paid amazing fees to show up. They spend their time traveling and getting booked all over the country and they are making a handsome living from it. They are providing real value to these organizations and the people paying them respect what they do.

That is the type of speaker that you want to be. Remember that your time is valuable and you are in business to make money, not lose it.

Getting booked to speak is cool, but getting paid to speak is way cooler, don't you agree?

Day 18: Today's Thought

Don't wait. The time will never be just right.
Napoleon Hill

Day 19: Looking Back

I am LA-bound next week and while I am there I have reserved some consulting days with some of my coaching clients on the West Coast, so this will be an action-packed trip that I am looking forward to very much.

We'll be looking back on the year so far and making plans for what needs to be done to stay on track. So, as you look at where you are now, can you honestly say you are happy with your progress so far?

It doesn't matter if you are falling short of your goals, it matters that you moved toward them in some fashion or form.

Or, looking back, is this year so far another flop for you? Another year where you started out with big plans and a big bang only to fizzle out someplace down the line?

Unfortunately this is a vicious cycle and pattern that many people fall into.

Most of the time this pattern repeats itself until you realize you have to do something different from what you have been doing because... it ain't working!

Being a solopreneur does not mean that you have to do everything by yourself.

It means you have the ability to leverage other resources to assist you and you have the ability to learn from someone who holds you accountable, pushes you and forces you to "show up" and perform.

Day 22: Today's Action

Identify a new skill that will help you in your business – such as copywriting – and make a commitment to spending time every day working on it.

Day 23: Why You are Worth the Investment

I just spent an hour trying to get someplace it should have taken me no time to get to; we are experiencing some major flooding in our area and I had to come back home due to all the closed roads.

I have a hair appointment that I MUST get to today, I have been hiding from the public because my hair is a disaster and, when I have been going out, I have been hiding it under a hat.

If I have to SWIM to the hair salon, that is what I am going to do! LOL.

So today, someone sent me a nasty email letting me know that they were not contributing a dime to my bank account.

This is a person who signed up on my list and has been on it for a while.

I guess they finally got fed up with me launching all my products and services to help entrepreneurs get to the level they deserve and decided to "let me have it."

But let me tell you what this misguided person REALLY has going on.

First, the nasty message was sent from their government agency email meaning they were strapped to their desk at work, most likely frustrated. I can empathize; they probably have bigger dreams for themselves.

Second, the mindset is clearly off and here is why. Anyone who opts into my list does so on a voluntary basis and most likely is someone interested in self-investment and entrepreneurship.

I am an entrepreneurial and business coach who shows others how I was able to build a million dollar business by focusing on sales and marketing strategies. Those who my message resonates with and who want to jump on board, I will gladly give all that I have got.

But those who look at their own self-investment as an investment in ME instead have got it all wrong.

This means the focus is on my business and what I have built and somehow that bothers them.

Jealousy? Maybe, but what I find most is that people are frustrated with their own situations and so they lash out at others.

- If you want to be a doctor, you must make the investment to go to medical school.
- If you want to be a lawyer, you must invest in law school.
- If you want to be a successful entrepreneur, you invest in a mentor or coach who can lead you there.

At the end of the day, when someone has knowledge that you do not have that can move you towards your desired goal, you make the decision to invest in getting it. That's what I do all the time, don't you?

I remember being at work too, not wanting to be there and feeling chained to my desk. But when I made the decision to learn how to invest in real estate, I didn't get mad at the coaches who taught real estate investing; instead I wrote them a check to learn how to do what they were doing.

When I wanted to learn more about marketing and profitable live events, I wrote James Malinchak a check to learn how.

I didn't get upset at him being a multi-millionaire and feel as if I was giving him anything he didn't already have; it was an investment in ME because I believe in myself.

And guess what? If I hadn't written him a check, he would STILL be a millionaire and I would STILL not have the knowledge I needed. So I ask you, who is WINNING when you refuse to pay someone who is already successful with or without you to learn a skill you don't have?

Don't ever let your frustration take over, always believe in yourself enough to know that you are worthy of better things and that the people who can help you get there are actually your allies and not your enemy!

Just ask all my coaching students who are shocked and amazed to see that I am their biggest cheerleader in both life and in business!

This one mindset shift alone can open up a brand new world!

Day 24: Today's Thought

The important thing is to not be afraid to take a chance. Remember, the greatest failure is to not try. Once you find something you love to do, be the best at doing it.
Debbi Fields

Day 25: Next Year!

Ok, so I can't take this phrase anymore!

"Next year."

Do you know that is like the #1 phrase people use when they want to be a part of something, but talk themselves out of it?

How many times have you looked at a goal you intended to accomplish and said "next year"?

Or maybe you wanted to attend a great event but ended up saying "next year." Perhaps you were supposed to start a healthier eating regimen and once again, you said "next year."

It's easy to let yourself off the hook year after year, but if you look at how many times you have said "next year" it could just very well be that five years have passed and you still haven't made that quantum leap yet!

In my circle, I can't get away with that. I am surrounded by people who would never allow me to even go there and I don't let anyone that I coach or mentor get away with that either.

The fact of the matter is this. Many people are self-motivated, but to stay in that mode 365 days a year 24/7 is unrealistic and impossible. Even the most HIGHLY motivated person you know needs a kick in the butt to stay on course.

Wouldn't it be great if we could do it all alone and didn't need anyone else? Unfortunately that isn't the case. We are our own worst enemy sometimes. And we like to blame others for our faults and issues, don't we?

When the reality of it all is that we are usually the ONLY one standing in our way. Making excuses why we aren't progressing or blaming the economy. It's not until we come clean and get real with ourselves that we will be ready to make a change.

It's time to live for YOU! Jump out there and tackle those life goals so that you never again have to say that tired old worn out phrase… "NEXT YEAR."

Day 26: Today's Action

Write down 10 things that will be better in your business and in your life 12 months from now.

Day 29: Planning Ahead

I am hopping on a plane this morning to Vegas to go and work with my coach and mentor on mapping out my business goals and plans for next year.

This will be an intense day of digging deep, being honest and making some real assessments of what's working, what's not and the FASTEST way to the cash!

Then as soon as I get back I am gearing up to host my second meeting with my high level Platinum Mastermind coaching students where we will gather together all weekend and dive into their businesses. I love my mastermind group; these ladies are serious about not wasting another year in their business trying to figure things out alone.

So WHAT will separate the people who actually make their goals a reality from the people who never reach their goals?

- STRONG DESIRE! The person who is sick and tired of being sick and tired will stick to their guns. The person who just kind of knows it's the "in" thing to set goals each year will talk about it, but never take the necessary actions to make it a reality.
- STRENGTH! Nobody said it was easy to form and stick to new success habits. Doing something new is uncomfortable to most people, but without it you will stay stagnant. Change is scary, and seems like a big hassle. As humans we love to stay in our nice, safe comfort zone. But staying comfortable means you have made the decision to stay stuck. You have decided not to live bigger and you have decided not to go for your dreams. And who REALLY wants that?
- SO WHAT! The so what factor is what separates people who move towards their goals from those who do not. So what if I don't do it right the first time? So what if I have some failures? So what if it is not perfect? So what if people talk about me?

People with big dreams and goals know that they are subjecting themselves to the opinions of others, but they do not care. Trying to live your life for other people is a game you will never win, so don't waste any more time doing it!

Ask yourself these questions...

- Do you have a strong desire to make this a better year than the last?

- Do you have the strength to endure stepping out of your comfort zone so that you can grow?

- Do you have what it takes to say "So what?" and take action regardless if it is perfect or not?

If the answer is yes, then you are well on your way to making the next 12 months your best ever! This could just very well be the year you actually make your dreams a reality.

Day 30: Today's Thought

Now, get out there and kick ass!
Stella McCartney

Looking Back and Looking Forward

What are the top five things you have learned this month?

1.

2.

3.

4.

5.

What are the top five actions you will take next month?

1.

2.

3.

4.

5.

FINAL THOUGHTS

I hope you've enjoyed this journey through my year and that it's given you a new insight into the Superwoman Lifestyle.

As I said at the start of this book, I didn't publish this diary to imply that there is anything special about me and the way I live.

I wanted to share what I was experiencing and to show how being a Superwoman is not some fancy theory but is something practical that touches everything we do each day.

Experiencing the Superwoman Lifestyle is about the simple choices you make every day and it's about taking advantage of the opportunities available to you.

In telling you about the daily experiences in my life – personal and business – I wanted to show you how I apply the Superwoman principles to everything that I do.

I also shared some quotes that inspire me, and recommended some regular actions you can take to make sure you get the Superwoman habit. The best way to get started is to make sure you have read my first book.

It's called *"The Superwoman Lifestyle Blueprint: The Ultimate Woman's Guide to Embracing Her Strengths, Defining Her All, and Living the Life She Was Born to Live in Business, Beauty & Balance."*

These three pillars are the keys to living the life you want to live:

- **Business**: Too many women fail to get the results they are capable of in business due to fear, self-doubt and the lack of knowledge on how to pull it all together

- **Beauty**: If you don't feel good about yourself on the inside and the outside, you will be limited in what you can achieve

- **Balance**: Many women hold back on their own dreams because they give too much time to others and neglect themselves

In the *"Superwoman Lifestyle Blueprint"*, I share a five-step process designed to help you start living the Superwoman Lifestyle right away.

As you are reading this book, you probably already have what you need to start living the Superwoman Lifestyle. You just need to identify it, unleash it, embrace it and then learn how to work it.

My mission is to inspire you and show you how it is possible for you. So please make sure you read my first book and stay connected.

I hope what you've seen in this book will inspire you to join me on that journey. Congratulations for taking this important step and I wish you all the success you deserve.

Visit us at www.SuperWomanLifestyle.com to join thousands of progressive women like yourself and become part of this phenomenal movement that is transforming lives one day at a time.

WHAT PEOPLE ARE SAYING ABOUT VICKI

Vicki helped me to create a brand within a market that is very crowded. She found a way to differentiate my business and make me stand out, while staying authentic to myself. I am so excited about the new direction of my business and now feel totally comfortable marketing myself!

Charisa Pruitt
The Seo Alliance Team
www.TheSeoAllianceTeam.com

I needed help with my business and decided to work with Vicki Irvin. The information I learned was amazing; she helped me put a new business model and strategy in place that resulted in instant profit just two weeks later! I can't wait to implement all of the other things I got from her!

Tracye McQuirter
Author, Coach
www.ByAnyGreensNecessary.com

Watching Vicki made me realize what was really possible. I came to her event with one idea, but then left and changed directions completely. I took her "riches in niches" and branding messages and put together an offline ad campaign based on some of the concepts from the materials and brought in a nice 5-figure income in month one! Thanks Vicki!

Karen Philippin-Kilpatrick
Attorney
www.SoFlowLaw.com

Vicki Irvin is more than a marketing coach – she is the premier Master Marketing Strategist. Vicki's wealth of knowledge and marketing experience is incredible. Vicki immediately pinpointed areas of improvement for my website and suggested tips to increase my clientele. I immediately implemented her recommendations. Nearly three weeks later, I am seeing amazing results. To top it off, her professionalism, exceptional communication style, and one-on-one sessions made the experience one to remember. Without doubt, Vicki Irvin is the best and unparalleled to others in the marketing arena.

Nisha Parker
Author, Coach
www.SynergyLounge.org

I have increased my net worth by $300,000 since June 2008 using Vicki Irvin's principles and have made more than $100,000 in profit in just the first 12 months. Vicki only teaches win-win solutions for all parties and with the highest moral and ethical standards for her students. This is the only way to do business and it will give you the personal satisfaction that you are making a positive difference in the business community. Simply amazing!

Cynthia Gordan-Nicks
CGN Investment
www.NickBuysHouses.com

Vicki's branding experience was the most productive step towards marketing my business expertise that I have taken so far. She developed a branded Five Step S.P.A.C.E. Transformation System that clearly conveys my value to prospective customers. It's brilliant! Thank you, Vicki!

Mary Roberts
Successful Spaces
www.SuccessfulStudentEnvironments.com

I recently worked with Vicki on building my Brand and I am thrilled! I am currently on the TV show America Now and also in production for another TV show coming out soon. Most recently I got booked to appear on the TV show "The Doctors" to premiere my new fitness product "Fi-Danz" in front of millions of people. Vicki helped me develop an appealing Brand that conveys who I am in the fitness industry and as a result, mega media opportunities are coming my way! There is nobody better than Vicki!

Basheerah Amad
Celebrity Fitness Trainer
www.BasheerahAmad.com

Vicki Irvin has been the "find" of the decade for me. With her coaching, mentoring and support, I have been able to complete my first book, speak on stage at live events, and I am now in the process of creating my affiliate marketing coaching program for women entrepreneurs! It's awesome when you can find the right person to hone your skills and talents so that you can enrich the lives of others with your gifts. Thanks Vicki.

Kimberly Davis,
Author, Speaker, Coach
www.KimADavis

Vicki is not only brilliant and talented; she's a pleasure to work with. She has an amazing ability to look at all the work and effort you have already done and find your brand within your own words. Her passion for setting her clients apart from the rest truly shows.

Cheryl Paulsen
Cheryl Paulsen Coaching
www.CherylPaulsenCoaching.com

The inspiration, perspective – and time to think – from Vicki Irvin's event led me to make a major decision absolutely key to growing my business — hiring a communications and marketing expert. For too long, I was trying to do this important job on my own. It was only ONE of many revelations I had that I acted on from Vicki's event that has profoundly and positively affected my business.

Debbie Phillips
Women on Fire®
www.BeAWomanOnFire.com

I was blown away by the marketing strategies and techniques that I learned from Vicki. Even though I have an MBA, I learned brand new marketing strategies I had never heard before because you can't learn this from a textbook. You get real-life proven techniques from entrepreneurs who have done it and are still doing it! Not theory and academic marking ideas. Vicki introduces women to the proven marketing systems, strategies and concepts that successful entrepreneurs are using today to earn six figures and seven figures!

Adwoa M. Jones
Founder, Crystal Clear Interviews
www.PrepareforYourInterview.com

It has been a pleasure being one of Vicki Irvin's coaching clients. I've been gleaning from her since 2008. She is patient, she is thorough but most of all she is good at what she does. I love the fact that she gives individualized attention. The strategies I learned are the foundation of success for every hopeful entrepreneur. I'm glad to have made an investment in my education because the principles that Vicki is teaching will take my business to the next level & beyond!

Shelly King
Destine 4 Change, LLC
www.Destine4Change.com